PAROCHIAL AND PLAIN SERMONS

VOLUME VIII

CARDINAL NEWMAN'S WORKS.

Parochial and Plain Sermons. Edited by the Rev. W. J. Copeland, B.D. 8 vols. *Crown 8vo.*

Selections, adapted to the Seasons of the Ecclesiastical Year, from the 'Parochial and Plain Sermons.' Edited by the Rev. W. J. Copeland, B.D. *Crown 8vo.*

Sermons bearing upon subjects of the Day. Edited by the Rev. W. J. Copeland, B.D. *Crown 8vo.*

Lectures on the Doctrine of Justification. *Crown 8vo.*

Fifteen Sermons preached before the University of Oxford, between 1826 and 1843. *Crown 8vo.*

Apologia pro Vitâ Suâ. *Crown 8vo.*

The Idea of a University Defined and Illustrated. *Crown 8vo.*

Historical Sketches. 3 vols. *Crown 8vo.*

The Arians of the Fourth Century. *Crown 8vo.*

Select Treatises of St. Athanasius in Controversy with the Arians. Freely Translated. 2 vols. *Crown 8vo.*

Discussions and Arguments on various subjects. *Crown 8vo.*

An Essay on the Development of Christian Doctrine. *Crown 8vo.*

Certain Difficulties felt by Anglicans in Catholic Teaching Considered. 2 vols.

The Via Media of the Anglican Church, illustrated in Lectures, etc. 2 vols. *Crown 8vo.*

Essays Critical and Historical. 2 vols. *Crown 8vo.*

Essays on Biblical and on Ecclesiastical Miracles. *Crown 8vo.*

An Essay in aid of a Grammar of Assent.

Present Position of Catholics in England. *Crown 8vo.*

Callista : a Tale of the Third Century. *Crown 8vo.*

The Dream of Gerontius. 16mo.

Verses on Various Occasions. *Crown 8vo.*

LONDON : LONGMANS, GREEN, & CO.

PAROCHIAL AND PLAIN SERMONS

By JOHN HENRY NEWMAN, B.D.

FORMERLY VICAR OF ST. MARY'S, OXFORD

IN EIGHT VOLUMES

VOL. VIII.

NEW EDITION

LONDON

LONGMANS, GREEN, AND CO.

AND NEW YORK: 15 EAST 16TH STREET

1891

CONTENTS.

SERMON V.

Curiosity a Temptation to Sin.

SERMON VI.

Miracles no Remedy for Unbelief.

SERMON VII.

Josiah, a Pattern for the Ignorant.

SERMON VIII.

Inward Witness to the Truth of the Gospel.

SERMON I.

Reverence in Worship.

"Samuel ministered before the Lord, being a child, girded with a linen ephod."—1 SAMUEL ii. 18.

SAMUEL, viewed in his place in sacred history, that is, in the course of events which connect Moses with Christ, appears as a great ruler and teacher of his people; this is his prominent character. He was the first of the prophets; yet, when we read the sacred narrative itself, in which his life is set before us, I suppose those passages are the more striking and impressive which represent him, in the office which belonged to him by birth, as a Levite, or minister of God. He was taken into God's special service from the first; he lived in His Temple; nay, while yet a child, he was honoured with the apparel of a sacred function, as the text tells us, "he ministered before the Lord, being a child, girded with a linen ephod."

His mother had "given him unto the Lord all the

[VIII]

B

days of his life [1]," by a solemn vow before his birth;
and in him, if in any one, were fulfilled the words of
the Psalmist, "Blessed are they that dwell in Thy
house, they will be always praising Thee [2]."

Such a constant abode in God's house would make
common minds only familiar with holy things, and
irreverent; but where God's grace is present in the
heart, the effect is the reverse; which we might be sure
would happen in the case of Samuel. "The Lord was
with him," we are told; and therefore the more the
outward signs of that Lord met his eye, the more
reverent he became, not the more presuming. The
more he acquainted himself with God, the greater
would be his awe and holy fear.

Thus the first notice we have of his ministering before
the Lord, reminds us of the decency and gravity necessary at all times, and in all persons, in approaching
Him. "He ministered before the Lord, being a child,
girded with a linen ephod." His mother had made him
yearly a little coat for his common use, but in Divine
Service he wore, not this, but a garment which would
both express, and impress upon him, reverence.

And, in like manner, in his old age, when Saul sent
to seek David at Naioth, where Samuel was, his messengers found Samuel and the prophets under him all in
decent order. "They saw the company of prophets
prophesying, and Samuel over them." And this was so

---

[1] Sam. i. 11.   [2] Ps. lxxxiv. 4.

impressive a sight, that it became an instrument of God's supernatural power towards them, and they prophesied also.

On the other hand, if we would have an example of the want of this reverence, we have it in Saul himself, the reprobate king, who, when he was on his way to Naioth, and was visited by God's Holy Spirit, did not thereupon receive the garment of salvation, nor was clothed in righteousness, but behaved himself in an unseemly wild way, as one whose destitution and shame were but detected by the visitation. He stript off his clothes and prophesied before Samuel, and lay down in that state all that day and all that night.

This difference we see even at this day:—of persons professing religion, some are like Samuel, some like Saul; some (as it were) cast off their garments and prophesy in disorder and extravagance; others minister before the Lord, "girded with a linen ephod," with "their loins girt and their lamps burning," like men awfully expecting the coming of their great and glorious Judge. By the latter, I mean the true children of the Holy Catholic Church; by the former, I mean heretics and schismatics.

There have ever been from the first these two kinds of Christians—those who belonged to the Church, and those who did not. There never was a time since the Apostles' day, when the Church was not; and there never was a time but men were to be found who preferred some other way of worship to the Church's way. These two kinds of professed Christians ever have been —Church Christians, and Christians not of the Church; and it is remarkable, I say, that while, on the one hand, reverence for sacred things has been a characteristic of Church Christians on the whole, so, want of reverence has been the characteristic on the whole of Christians not of the Church. The one have prophesied after the figure of Samuel, the other after the figure of Saul.

Of course there are many exceptions to this remark in the case of individuals. Of course I am not speaking of inconsistent persons and exceptional cases, in the Church, or out of it; but of those who act up to what they profess. I mean that zealous, earnest, and faithful members of the Church have generally been reverent; and zealous, earnest, and faithful members of other religious bodies have generally been irreverent. Again, after all, there will be real exceptions in the case of individuals which we cannot account for; but I mean that, *on the whole*, it will be found that reverence is one of the marks or notes of the Church; true though it may be that some particular individuals, who have kept apart from it, have not been without a reverential spirit notwithstanding.

Indeed so natural is the connexion between a reverential spirit in worshipping God, and faith in God, that the wonder only is, how any one can for a moment imagine he has faith in God, and yet allow himself to

be irreverent towards Him. To believe in God, is to
believe the being and presence of One who is All-holy,
and All-powerful, and All-gracious; how can a man
really believe thus of Him, and yet make free with
Him? it is almost a contradiction in terms. Hence
even heathen religions have ever considered faith and
reverence identical. To believe, and not to revere, to
worship familiarly, and at one's ease, is an anomaly
and a prodigy unknown even to false religions, to say
nothing of the true one. Not only the Jewish and
Christian religions, which are directly from God, inculcate the spirit of " reverence and godly fear," but those
other religions which have existed, or exist, whether in
the East or the South, inculcate the same. Worship,
forms of worship—such as bowing the knee, taking
off the shoes, keeping silence, a prescribed dress, and the
like—are considered as necessary for a due approach to
God. The whole world, differing about so many things,
differing in creed and rule of life, yet agree in this—
that God being our Creator, a certain self-abasement
of the whole man is the duty of the creature; that He
is in heaven, we upon earth; that He is All-glorious,
and we worms of the earth and insects of a day.

But those who have separated from the Church of
Christ have in this respect fallen into greater than
pagan error. They may be said to form an exception
to the concordant voice of a whole world, always and
every where; they break in upon the unanimous suf-

frage of mankind, and determine, at least by their conduct, that reverence and awe are not primary religious
duties. They have considered that in some way or
other, either by God's favour or by their own illumination, they are brought so near to God that they have
no need to fear at all, or to put any restraint upon their
words or thoughts when addressing Him. They have
considered awe to be superstition, and reverence to be
slavery. They have learnt to be familiar and free with
sacred things, as it were, on principle. I think this is
really borne out by facts, and will approve itself to
inquirers as true in substance, however one man will
differ from another in the words in which he would
express the fact itself.

Samuel was a little child who had never fallen away
from God, but by His grace had ever served Him. Let
us take a very different instance, the instance of a penitent sinner as set before us in the parable of the Publican and Pharisee. I need hardly say which of the two
was the most pleasing to God—the Publican; whereas
the Pharisee was not accepted by Him. Now what did
the Pharisee do? He did not even go so far as to
behave in an unseemly, extravagant way: he was grave
and solemn, and yet what he did was enough to displease God, because he took too much upon himself, and
made too much of himself. Though grave and solemn,
he was not reverent; he spoke in a haughty, proud way,
and made a long sentence, thanking God that he was

not as other men are, and despising the Publican. Such was the behaviour of the Pharisee; but the Publican behaved very differently. Observe how he came to worship God; "he stood afar off; he lift not up so much as his eyes unto heaven, but smote upon his breast, saying, God be merciful to me a sinner[1]." You see his words were few, and almost broken, and his whole conduct humble and reverent; he felt that God was in heaven, he upon earth, God All-holy and Almighty, and he a poor sinner.

Now all of us are sinners, all of us have need to come to God as the Publican did; every one, if he does but search his heart, and watch his conduct, and try to do his duty, will find himself to be full of sins which provoke God's wrath. I do not mean to say that all men are equally sinners; some are wilful sinners, and of them there is no hope, till they repent; others sin, but they try to avoid sinning, pray to God to make them better, and come to Church to be made better; but all men are quite sinners enough to make it their duty to behave as the Publican. Every one ought to come into Church as the Publican did, to say in his heart, "Lord, I am not worthy to enter this sacred place; my only plea for coming is the merits of Jesus Christ my Saviour." When, then, a man enters Church, as many do, carelessly and familiarly, thinking of himself, not of God, sits down coldly and at his ease, either

[1] Luke xviii. 13.

does not say a prayer at all, or merely hides his face for form's sake, sitting all the while, not standing or kneeling; then looks about to see who is in the Church, and who is not, and makes himself easy and comfortable in his seat, and uses the kneeler for no other purpose than to put his feet upon; in short, comes to Church as a place, not of meeting God and His holy Angels, but of seeing what is to be seen with the bodily eyes, and hearing what is to be heard with the bodily ears, and then goes and gives his judgment about the sermon freely, and says, "I do not like this or that," or "This is a good argument, but that is a bad one," or "I do not like this person so much as that," and so on; I mean when a man acts in all respects as if he was at home, and not in God's House,—all I can say is, that he ventures to do in God's presence what neither Cherubim nor Seraphim venture to do, for they veil their faces, and, as if not daring to address God, praise Him to each other, in few words, and those continually repeated, saying, Holy, holy, holy, Lord God of Sabaoth.

What I have said has been enough to suggest what it is to serve God acceptably, viz. " with reverence and godly fear," as St. Paul says. We must not aim at forms for their own sake, but we must keep in mind where we are, and then forms will come into our service naturally. We must in all respects act as if we saw God; that is, if we believe that God is here, we shall keep silence; we shall not laugh, or talk, or whisper during the Service, as many young persons do; we shall not gaze about us. We shall follow the example set us by the Church itself. I mean, as the words in which we pray in Church are not our own, neither will our looks, or our postures, or our thoughts, be our own. We shall, in the prophet's words, not "do our own ways" there, nor "find our own pleasure," nor "speak our own words;" in imitation of all Saints before us, including the Holy Apostles, who never spoke their own words in solemn worship, but either those which Christ taught them, or which the Holy Ghost taught them, or which the Old Testament taught them. This is the reason why we always pray from a book in Church; the Apostles said to Christ, "Lord, teach us to pray," and our Lord graciously gave them the prayer called the Lord's Prayer. For the same reason we too use the Lord's Prayer, and we use the Psalms of David and of other holy men, and hymns which are given us in Scripture, thinking it better to use the words of inspired Prophets than our own. And for the same reason we use a number of short petitions, such as "Lord, have mercy upon us," "O Lord, save the Queen," "O Lord, open Thou our lips," and the like, not using many words, or rounding our sentences, or allowing ourselves to enlarge in prayer.

Thus all we do in Church is done on a principle of *reverence;* it is done with the thought that we are in God's presence. But irreverent persons, not understand-

ing this, when they come into Church, and find nothing
there of a striking kind, when they find every thing
is read from a book, and in a calm, quiet way, and still
more, when they come a second and a third time, and
find every thing just the same, over and over again,
they are offended and tired. "There is nothing," they
say, "to rouse or interest them." They think God's
service dull and tiresome, if I may use such words;
for they do not come to Church to honour God, but
to please themselves. They want something new. They
think the prayers are long, and wish that there was
more preaching, and that in a striking oratorical way,
with loud voice and florid style. And when they observe that the worshippers in Church are serious and
subdued in their manner, and will not look, and speak,
and move as much at their ease as out of doors, or in
their own houses, then (if they are very profane) they
ridicule them, as weak and superstitious. Now is it not
plain that those who are thus tired, and wearied, and
made impatient by our sacred services below, would most
certainly get tired and wearied with heaven above?
because there the Cherubim and Seraphim "rest not
day and night," saying, "Holy, holy, holy, Lord God
Almighty." Such as this, too, will be the way of the
Saints in glory, for we are told that there will be a
great voice of much people saying, Alleluia; and again
they said Alleluia; and the four-and-twenty elders said
Alleluia; and a voice of many waters and of mighty

thunderings said Alleluia. Such, too, was our Lord's way, when in His agony He three times repeated the same words, "Thy will, not Mine, be done." It is the delight of all holy beings, who stand around the Throne, to use one and the same form of worship; they are not tired, it is ever new pleasure to them to say the words anew. They are never tired; but surely all those persons would be soon tired of hearing them, instead of taking part in their glorious chant, who are wearied of Church now, and seek for something more attractive and rousing.

Let all persons, then, know for certain, and be assured beforehand, that if they come to Church to have their hearts put into strange and new forms, and their feelings moved and agitated, they come for what they will not find. We wish them to join Saints and Angels in worshipping God; to say with the Seraphim, "Holy Lord God of Sabaoth;" to say with the Angels, "Glory to God in the highest, and in earth peace, good-will towards men;" to say after our Lord and Saviour, "Our Father, which art in heaven," and what follows; to say with St. Mary, "My soul doth magnify the Lord;" with St. Simeon, "Lord, now lettest Thou Thy servant depart in peace;" with the Three Children who were cast into the fiery furnace, "O all ye works of the Lord, bless ye the Lord, praise Him, and magnify Him for ever;" with the Apostles, "I believe in God the Father Almighty, Maker of heaven and earth; and in Jesus Christ His only Son our Lord; and in the Holy

Ghost." We wish to read to them words of inspired Scripture, and to explain its doctrine to them soberly after its pattern. This is what we wish them to say, again and again: "Lord, have mercy;" "We beseech Thee to hear us, O Lord;" "Good Lord, deliver us;" "Glory be to the Father, and to the Son, and to the Holy Ghost." All holy creatures are praising God continually—we hear them not, still they are praising Him and praying to Him. All the Angels, the glorious company of the Apostles, the goodly fellowship of the Prophets, the noble army of Martyrs, the Holy Church universal, all good men all over the earth, all the spirits and souls of the righteous, all our friends who have died in God's faith and fear, all are praising and praying to God: we come to Church to join them; our voices are very feeble, our hearts are very earthly, our faith is very weak. We do not deserve to come, surely not;—consider what a great favour it is to be allowed to join in the praises and prayers of the City of the Living God, we being such sinners;—we should not be allowed to come at all but for the merits of our Lord and Saviour. Let us firmly look at the Cross, that is the token of our salvation. Let us ever remember the sacred Name of Jesus, in which devils were cast out of old time. These are the thoughts with which we should come to Church; and if we come a little before the Service begins, and want something to think about, we may look, not at who are coming in and when, but at the building itself, which will remind us of many good things; or we may look into the Prayer Book for such passages as the 84th Psalm, which runs thus: "O how amiable are Thy dwellings, Thou Lord of hosts! my soul hath a desire and longing to enter into the Courts of the Lord: my heart and my flesh rejoice in the Living God."

Such will be our conduct and our thoughts in Church, if we be true Christians; and I have been giving this description of them, not only for the sake of those who are not reverent, but for the sake of those who try to be so,—for the sake of all of us who try to come to Church soberly and quietly, that we may know why we do so, and may have an answer if any one asks us. Such will be our conduct even when we are out of Church. I mean, those who come to Church again and again, in this humble and heavenly way, will find the effect of it, through God's mercy, in their daily walk. When Moses came down from Mount Sinai, where he had been forty days and forty nights, his face quite shone and dazzled the people, so that he was obliged to put a veil over it. Such is the effect of God's grace on those who come to Church in faith and love; their mode of acting and talking, their very manner and behaviour, show they have been in God's presence. They are ever sober, cheerful, modest, serious, and earnest. They do not disgrace their profession, they do not take God's Name in vain, they do not use passionate language, they do not lie, they do not jest in an unseemly way, they do not use shameful words, they keep their mouth; they have kept their mouth in Church, and avoided rashness, so they are enabled to keep it at home. They have bright, smiling, pleasant faces. They do not wear a mock gravity, and, like the hypocrites whom Christ speaks of, make themselves sad countenances, but they are easy and natural, and without meaning it cannot help showing in their look, and voice, and manner, that they are God's dear children, and have His grace within them. They are civil and obliging, kind and friendly; not envious or jealous, not quarrelsome, not spiteful or resentful, not selfish, not covetous, not niggardly, not lovers of the world, not afraid of the world, not afraid of what man can do against them.

Such are they who worship God in spirit and in truth in Church; they love Him and they fear Him. And, besides those who profess to love without fearing, there are two sorts of persons who fall short; first, and worst, those who neither fear nor love God; and, secondly, those who fear Him, but do not love Him. There are, every where, alas! some bold, proud, discontented persons, who, as far as they dare, speak against religion altogether; they do not come to Church, or if they come, come to see about what is going on, not to worship. These are those who neither love nor fear; but the more common sort of persons are they who have a sort of fear of God without the love of Him, who feel and know that some things are right, and others wrong, yet do not adhere to the right; who are conscious they sin from time to time, and that wilfully, who have an uneasy conscience, who fear to die; who have, indeed, a sort of serious feeling about sacred things, who reverence the Church and its Ordinances, who would be shocked at open impiety, who do not make a mock at Baptism, much less at the Holy Communion, but, still, who have not the heart to love and obey God. This, I fear, my brethren, may be the state of some of you. See to it, that you are clear from the sin of knowing and confessing what is your duty, and yet not doing it. If you be such, and make no effort to become better; if you do not come to Church honestly, for God's grace to make you better, and seriously strive to be better and to do your duty more thoroughly, it will profit you nothing to be ever so reverent in your manner, and ever so regular in coming to Church. God hates the worship of the mere lips; He requires the worship of the heart. A person may bow, and kneel, and look religious, but he is not at all the nearer heaven, unless he tries to obey God in all things, and to do his duty. But if he does honestly strive to obey God, then his outward manner will be reverent also; decent forms will become natural to him; holy ordinances, though coming to him from the Church, will at the same time come (as it were) from his heart; they will be part of himself, and he will as little think of dispensing with them as he would dispense with his ordinary apparel, nay, as he could dispense with tongue or hand in speaking or doing. This is the true way of doing devotional service; not to have feelings without acts, or acts without feelings; but both to do and to feel;—to see that our hearts and bodies are both sanctified together, and become one; the heart ruling our limbs, and making the whole man serve Him, who has redeemed the whole man, body as well as soul.

SERMON II.

Divine Calls.

"And the Lord came, and stood, and called as at other times, Samuel, Samuel. Then Samuel answered, Speak ; for Thy servant heareth.'
—1 SAMUEL iii. 10.

IN the narrative of which these words form part, we have a remarkable instance of a Divine call, and the manner in which it is our duty to meet it. Samuel was from a child brought to the house of the Lord ; and in due time he was called to a sacred office, and made a prophet. He was called, and he forthwith answered the call. God said, "Samuel, Samuel." He did not understand at first who called, and what was meant ; but on going to Eli he learned who spoke, and what his answer should be. So when God called again, he said, " Speak, Lord, for Thy servant heareth." Here is prompt obedience.

Very different in its circumstances was St. Paul's call, but resembling Samuel's in this respect, that, when God called, he, too, promptly obeyed. When St. Paul heard the voice from heaven, he said at once, trembling and

c

astonished, " Lord, what wilt Thou have me to do[1]?"
This same obedient temper of his is stated or implied in
the two accounts which he himself gives of his miraculous conversion.   In the 22nd chapter he says, " And
I said, What shall I do, Lord?"   And in the 26th,
after telling King Agrippa what the Divine Speaker
said to him, he adds what comes to the same thing,
" Whereupon, O King Agrippa, *I was not disobedient*
unto the heavenly vision."   Such is the account given
us in St. Paul's case of that first step in God's gracious
dealings with him, which ended in his eternal salvation.
" Whom He did foreknow, He also did predestinate[2];"
—" whom He did predestinate, them He also called "—
here was the first act which took place in time—" and
whom He called, them He also justified; and whom He
justified, them He also glorified."   Such is the Divine
series of mercies; and you see that it was prompt obedience on St. Paul's part which carried on the first act
of Divine grace into the second, which knit together the
first mercy to the second.   " Whom He called, them
He also justified."   St. Paul was called when Christ
appeared to him in the way; he was justified when Ananias came to baptize him : and it was prompt obedience
which led him from his call to his baptism.   " Lord,
what wilt Thou have me to do?"   The answer was,
" Arise, and go into Damascus; and there it shall be
told thee of all things which are appointed for thee to

---

[1] Acts ix. 6.   [2] Rom. viii. 29.

do ." And when he came to Damascus, Ananias was sent to him by the same Lord who had appeared to him; and he reminded St. Paul of this when he came to him. The Lord had appeared for his call; the Lord appeared for his justification.

This, then, is the lesson taught us by St. Paul's conversion, promptly to obey the call. If we do obey it, to God be the glory, for He it is works in us. If we do not obey, to ourselves be all the shame, for sin and unbelief work in us. Such being the state of the case, let us take care to act accordingly,—being exceedingly alarmed lest we should *not* obey God's voice when He calls us, yet not taking praise or credit to ourselves if we *do* obey it. This has been the temper of all saints from the beginning—working out their salvation with fear and trembling, yet ascribing the work to Him who wrought in them to will and do of His good pleasure; obeying the call, and giving thanks to Him who calls, to Him who fulfils in them their calling. So much on the pattern afforded us by St. Paul.

Very different in its circumstances was Samuel's call, when a child in the temple, yet resembling St. Paul's in this particular,—that for our instruction the circumstance of his obedience to it is brought out prominently even in the words put into his mouth by Eli in the text. Eli taught him what to say, when called by the Divine voice. Accordingly, when " the Lord came, and

---

[1] Acts xxii. 10.

stood, and called as at other times, Samuel, Samuel. Then Samuel answered, Speak, Lord, for Thy servant heareth."

Such, again, is the temper of mind expressed by holy David in the 27th Psalm, "When Thou saidst, Seek ye My face, my heart said unto Thee, Thy face, Lord, will I seek."

And this temper, which in the above instances is illustrated in words spoken, is in the case of many other Saints in Scripture shown in word and deed; and, on the other hand, is illustrated negatively by being neglected in the case of others therein mentioned, who might have entered into life, and did not.

For instance, we read of the Apostles, that "Jesus, walking by the sea of Galilee, saw two brethren, Simon called Peter, and Andrew his brother, casting a net into the sea; for they were fishers. And He saith unto them, Follow Me, and I will make you fishers of men. *And* they *straightway* left their nets and followed Him [1]." Again; when He saw James and John with their father Zebedee, "He *called* them; and they *immediately left the ship, and their father,* and *followed* Him." And so of St. Matthew at the receipt of custom, "He said unto him, Follow Me; and he left all, rose up, and followed Him."

Again, we are told in St. John's Gospel, "Jesus would go forth into Galilee, and findeth Philip, and

[1] Matt. iv. 18—20.

saith unto Him, *Follow* Me." Again, " Philip findeth Nathanael," and in like manner says to him, " Come and see." " Jesus saw Nathanael coming unto Him, and saith of him, Behold an Israelite indeed, in whom is no guile."

On the other hand, the young ruler shrunk from the call, and found it a hard saying, " If thou wilt be perfect, go and sell that thou hast, and give to the poor, and thou shalt have treasure in heaven; and come, and follow Me. But when the young man heard that saying, he went away sorrowful, for he had great possessions[1]." Others who seemed to waver, or rather who asked for some little delay from human feeling, were rebuked for want of promptitude in their obedience;— for time stays for no one; the word of call is spoken and is gone; if we do not seize the moment, it is lost. Christ was on His road heavenward. He walked by the sea of Galilee[2]; He " passed forth[3];" He " passed by[4];" He did not stop; all men must join Him, or He would be calling on others beyond them[5]. " He said to another, Follow Me. But he said, Lord, suffer me first to go and bury my father. Jesus said unto him, Let the dead bury their dead : but go thou and preach the kingdom of God. And another also said, Lord, I will follow Thee : but let me first go bid them farewell, which are at home at my house. And Jesus said unto

[1] Matt. xix. 21, 22.   [2] Matt. iv. 18.
[3] Matt. ix. 9.   [4] Mark ii. 14.   [5] Matt. xx. 6, 7.

him, No man, having put his hand to the plough, and looking back, is fit for the kingdom of God [1]."

Not unlike these last instances are the circumstances of the call of the great prophet Elisha, though he does not seem to have incurred blame from Elijah for his lingering on the thoughts of what he was leaving. " He found Elisha, the son of Shaphat, who was plough-ing . . . Elijah passed by him, and cast his mantle over him." He did not stay; he passed on, and Elisha was obliged to run after him. " And he left the oxen, and ran after Elijah, and said, Let me, I pray thee, kiss my father and my mother, and then I will follow thee." This the prophet allowed him to do, and after that " he arose and followed Elijah, and ministered unto him."

Or once more consider the circumstances of the call of Abraham, the father of all who believe. He was called from his father's house, but was not told whither. St. Paul was bid go to Damascus, and there he was to receive further directions. In like manner Abraham left his home for a land " that I *will* show thee [2]," says Almighty God. Accordingly he went out, " not know-ing whither he went." " Abram departed as the Lord had spoken unto him."

Such are the instances of Divine calls in Scripture, and their characteristic is this; to require instant obe-dience, and next to call us we know not to what; to call us on in the darkness. Faith alone can obey them.

[1] Luke ix. 59—62.   [2] Gen. xii. 1.

But it may be urged, How does this concern us now? We were all called to serve God in infancy, before we could obey or disobey; we found ourselves called when reason began to dawn; we have been called to a state of salvation, we have been living as God's servants and children, all through our time of trial, having been brought into it in infancy through Holy Baptism, by the act of our parents. Calling is not a thing future with us, but a thing past.

This is true in a very sufficient sense; and yet it is true also that the passages of Scripture which I have been quoting do apply to us still,—do concern us, and may warn and guide us in many important ways; as a few words will show.

For in truth we are not called once only, but many times; all through our life Christ is calling us. He called us first in Baptism; but afterwards also; whether we obey His voice or not, He graciously calls us still. If we fall from our Baptism, He calls us to repent; if we are striving to fulfil our calling, He calls us on from grace to grace, and from holiness to holiness, while life is given us. Abraham was called from his home, Peter from his nets, Matthew from his office, Elisha from his farm, Nathanael from his retreat; we are all in course of calling, on and on, from one thing to another, having no resting-place, but mounting towards our eternal rest, and obeying one command only to have another put upon us. He calls us again and again, in order to

justify us again and again,—and again and again, and
more and more, to sanctify and glorify us.

It were well if we understood this; but we are slow
to master the great truth, that Christ is, as it were,
walking among us, and by His hand, or eye, or voice,
bidding us follow Him. We do not understand that
His call is a thing which takes place now. We think
it took place in the Apostles' days; but we do not
believe in it, we do not look out for it in our own case.
We have not eyes to see the Lord; far different from
the beloved Apostle, who knew Christ even when the
rest of the disciples knew Him not. When He stood
on the shore after His resurrection, and bade them cast
the net into the sea, "that disciple whom Jesus loved
saith unto Peter, It is the Lord [1]."

Now what I mean is this: that they who are living
religiously, have from time to time truths they did not
know before, or had no need to consider, brought before
them forcibly; truths which involve duties, which are
in fact precepts, and claim obedience. In this and
such-like ways Christ calls us now. There is nothing
miraculous or extraordinary in His dealings with us.
He works through our natural faculties and circumstances of life. Still what happens to us in providence
is in all essential respects what His voice was to those
whom He addressed when on earth: whether He commands by a visible presence, or by a voice, or by our

[1] John xxi. 7.

consciences, it matters not, so that we feel it to be a command. If it is a command, it may be obeyed or disobeyed; it may be accepted as Samuel or St. Paul accepted it, or put aside after the manner of the young man who had great possessions.

And these Divine calls are commonly, from the nature of the case, sudden now, and as indefinite and obscure in their consequences as in former times. The accidents and events of life are, as is obvious, one special way in which the calls I speak of come to us; and they, as we all know, are in their very nature, and as the word accident implies, sudden and unexpected. A man is going on as usual; he comes home one day, and finds a letter, or a message, or a person, whereby a sudden trial comes on him, which, if met religiously, will be the means of advancing him to a higher state of religious excellence, which at present he as little comprehends as the unspeakable words heard by St. Paul in paradise. By a trial we commonly mean, a something which if encountered well, will confirm a man in his present way; but I am speaking of something more than this; of what will not only confirm him, but raise him into a high state of knowledge and holiness. Many persons will find it very striking on looking back on their past lives, to observe what different notions they entertained at different periods, of what Divine truth was, what was the way of pleasing God, and what things were allowable or not, what excellence was, and what happiness.

I do not scruple to say, that these differences may be as great as that which may be supposed to have existed between St. Peter's state of mind when quietly fishing on the lake, or Elisha's when driving his oxen, and that new state of mind of each of them when called to be Apostle or Prophet. Elisha and St. Peter indeed were also called to a new mode of life; that I am not speaking of. I am not speaking of cases when persons change their condition, their place in society, their pursuit, and the like; I am supposing them to remain pretty much the same as before in outward circumstances; but I say that many a man is conscious to himself of having undergone inwardly great changes of view as to what truth is and what happiness. Nor, again, am I speaking of changes so great, that a man reverses his former opinions and conduct. He may be able to see that there is a connexion between the two; that his former has led to his latter; and yet he may feel that after all they differ in kind; that he has got into a new world of thought, and measures things and persons by a different rule.

Nothing, indeed, is more wonderful and strange than the different views which different persons take of the same subject. Take any single fact, event, or existing thing which meets us in the world; what various remarks will be made on it by different persons! For instance, consider the different lights in which any single action, of a striking nature, is viewed by different persons; or consider the view of wealth or a wealthy man, taken by this or that class in the community; what different feelings does it excite —envy, or respect, or ridicule, or angry opposition, or indifference, or fear and compassion; here are states of mind in which different parties may regard it. These are broad differences; others are quite as real, though more subtle. Religion, for instance, may be reverenced by the soldier, the man of literature, the trader, the statesman, and the theologian; yet how very distinct their modes of reverencing it, and how separate the standard which each sets up in his mind! Well, all these various modes of viewing things cannot one and all be the best mode, even were they all good modes; but this even is not the case. Some are contrary to others; some are bad. But even of those that are on the whole good, some are but in part good, some are imperfect, some have much bad mixed with them; and only one is best. Only one is the truth and the perfect truth; and which that is, none know but those who are in possession of it, if even they. But God knows which it is; and towards that one and only Truth He is leading us forward. He is leading forward His redeemed, He is training His elect, one and all, to the one perfect knowledge and obedience of Christ; not, however, without their co-operation, but by means of calls which they are to obey, and which if they do not obey, they lose place, and fall behind in their heavenly course. He leads them forward from strength to strength, and from glory to glory, up the steps of the ladder whose top reacheth to heaven. We pass from one state of knowledge to another; we are introduced into a higher region from a lower, by listening to Christ's call and obeying it.

Perhaps it may be the loss of some dear friend or relative through which the call comes to us; which shows us the vanity of things below, and prompts us to make God our sole stay. We through grace do so in a way we never did before; and in the course of years, when we look back on our life, we find that that sad event has brought us into a new state of faith and judgment, and that we are as though other men from what we were. We thought, before it took place, that we were serving God, and so we were in a measure; but we find that, whatever our present infirmities may be, and however far we be still from the highest state of illumination, then at least we were serving the world under the show and the belief of serving God.

Or again, perhaps something occurs to force us to take a part for God or against Him. The world requires of us some sacrifice which we see we ought not to grant to it. Some tempting offer is made us; or some reproach or discredit threatened us; or we have to determine and avow what is truth and what is error. We are enabled to act as God would have us act; and we do so in much fear and perplexity. We do not see our way clearly; we do not see what is to follow from what we have done, and how it bears upon our general conduct and opinions : yet perhaps it has the most important bearings. That little deed, suddenly exacted of us, almost suddenly resolved on and executed, may be as though a gate into the second or third heaven—an entrance into a higher state of holiness, and into a truer view of things than we have hitherto taken.

Or again, we get acquainted with some one whom God employs to bring before us a number of truths which were closed on us before; and we but half understand them, and but half approve of them; and yet God seems to speak in them, and Scripture to confirm them. This is a case which not unfrequently occurs, and it involves a call " to follow on to know the Lord [1]."

Or again, we may be in the practice of reading Scripture carefully, and trying to serve God, and its sense may, as if suddenly, break upon us, in a way it never did before. Some thought may suggest itself to us, which is a key to a great deal in Scripture, or which suggests a great many other thoughts. A new light may be thrown on the precepts of our Lord and His Apostles. We may be able to enter into the manner of life of the early Christians, as recorded in Scripture, which before was hidden from us, and into the simple maxims on which Scripture bases it. We may be led

[1] Hosea vi. 3.

to understand that it is very different from the life
which men live now. Now knowledge is a call to
action : an insight into the way of perfection is a call
to perfection.

Once more, it may so happen that we find ourselves,
how or why we cannot tell, much more able to obey
God in certain respects than heretofore. Our minds
are so strangely constituted, it is impossible to say
whether it is from the growth of habit suddenly showing itself, or from an unusual gift of Divine grace
poured into our hearts, but so it is ; let our temptation
be to sloth, or irresolution, or worldly anxiety, or pride,
or to other more base and miserable sins, we may
suddenly find ourselves possessed of a power of self-
command which we had not before. Or again, we
may have a resolution grow on us to serve God more
strictly in His house and in private than heretofore.
This is a call to higher things ; let us beware lest we
receive the grace of God in vain. Let us beware of
lapsing back ; let us avoid temptation. Let us strive
by quietness and caution to cherish the feeble flame, and
shelter it from the storms of this world. God may be
bringing us into a higher world of religious truth ; let
us work with Him.

To conclude. Nothing is more certain in matter of
fact, than that some men do feel themselves called to
high duties and works, to which others are not called.
Why this is we do not know ; whether it be that those

who are not called. forfeit the call from having failed in
former trials, or have been called and have not followed;
or that though God gives baptismal grace to all, yet He
really does call some men by His free grace to higher
things than others; but so it is; this man sees sights
which that man does not see, has a larger faith, a more
ardent love, and a more spiritual understanding.   No
one has any leave to take another's lower standard of
holiness for his own.   It is nothing to us what others
are.   If God calls us to greater renunciation of the
world, and exacts a sacrifice of our hopes and fears, this
is our gain, this is a mark of His love for us, this is a
thing to be rejoiced in.   Such thoughts, when properly
entertained, have no tendency to puff us up; for if the
prospect is noble, yet the risk is more fearful.   While
we pursue high excellence, we walk among precipices,
and a fall is easy.   Hence the Apostle says, "Work out
your own salvation with fear and trembling, for it is
God that worketh in you[1]."   Again, the more men aim
at high things, the more sensitive perception they have
of their own shortcomings; and this again is adapted to
humble them especially.   We need not fear spiritual
pride then, in following Christ's call, if we follow it as
men in earnest.   Earnestness has no time to compare
itself with the state of other men; earnestness has too
vivid a feeling of its own infirmities to be elated at
itself.   Earnestness is simply set on doing God's will.

[1] Phil. ii. 12. 13.

It simply says, " Speak, Lord, for Thy servant heareth,"
" Lord, what wilt Thou have me to do?"   Oh that we
had more of this spirit!   Oh that we could take that
simple view of things, as to feel that the one thing
which lies before us is to please God!   What gain is it
to please the world, to please the great, nay, even to
please those whom we love, compared with this?   What
gain is it to be applauded, admired, courted, followed,
compared with this one aim, of not being disobedient to
a heavenly vision?   What can this world offer com-
parable with that insight into spiritual things, that
keen faith, that heavenly peace, that high sanctity,
that everlasting righteousness, that hope of glory, which
they have who in sincerity love and follow our Lord
Jesus Christ?

Let us beg and pray Him day by day to reveal Himself to our souls more fully; to quicken our senses; to
give us sight and hearing, taste and touch of the world
to come; so to work within us that we may sincerely
say, "Thou shalt guide me with Thy counsel, and after
that receive me to glory.   Whom have I in heaven but
Thee? and there is none upon earth that I desire in
comparison of Thee: my flesh and my heart faileth;
but God is the strength of my heart, and my portion for
ever."

SERMON III.

The Trial of Saul.

"And Saul said, Bring hither a burnt offering to me, and peace offerings. And he offered the burnt offering."—I SAMUEL xiii. 9.

WE are all on our trial. Every one who lives is on his trial, whether he will serve God or not. And we read in Scripture of many instances of the trials upon which Almighty God puts us His creatures. In the beginning, Adam, when he was first created, was put upon his trial. He was placed in a beautiful garden, he had every thing given him for his pleasure and comfort; he was created innocent and upright, and he had the great gift of the Holy Spirit given him to enable him to please God, and to attain to heaven. One thing alone he was forbidden—to eat of the tree of the knowledge of good and evil; this was his trial. If he did not eat of the fruit, he was to live; if he did, he was to die. Alas, he did eat of the fruit, and he did die. He was tried and found wanting; he fell; such was the end of *his* trial.

Many other trials, besides Adam's, are recorded in Scripture, and that for our warning and instruction; that we may be reminded that we too are on trial, that we may be encouraged by the examples of those who have stood their trial well and not fallen, and may be sobered and put on our guard by the instances of others who have fallen under their trial. Of these latter cases, Saul is one. Saul, of whom we have been reading in the course of this service [1], is an instance of a man whom God blessed and proved, as Adam before him, whom He put on his trial, and who, like Adam, was found wanting.

Now the history, I say, of this melancholy and awful fall is contained in the chapter which we have been reading, and from which the text is taken; and I will now attempt to explain to you its circumstances.

Saul was not born a king, or the son of a great family; he was a man of humble birth and circumstances, and he was raised by God's free grace to be the ruler and king of His people Israel. Samuel, God's prophet, revealed this to him, anointed him with oil, and after he became king, instructed him in his duty: and, moreover, put him on his trial. Now his trial was this. God's people, the Israelites, over whom Saul was appointed to reign, had been very much oppressed and harassed by their enemies round about; heathen nations, who hated the true God and His worship, rose and

[1] Fourth Sunday after Trinity.

fought against them; and of these nations the Philistines were the chief at that time. They overran the country, and brought the Israelites into captivity. They tyrannized over them, and to make sure that they should never be free, they even took away from them the means of forging weapons to fight with. "There was no smith found through all the land of Israel," says the chapter, "for the Philistines said, Lest the Hebrews (i. e. the Israelites) make them swords or spears. But all the Israelites went down to the Philistines, to sharpen every man his share, and his coulter, and his ax, and his mattock." Saul was raised up to throw off this heavy yoke, and to destroy the cruel oppressors of his people. He "chose him three thousand men, and with a third of them Jonathan, his son, smote the garrison of the Philistines which was in Geba."

Upon this, as was naturally to be supposed, these powerful enemies the Philistines became highly incensed, and assembled together a great army to chastise the insurgent people, their subjects as they would call them, who were making head against them. They had "thirty thousand chariots, and six thousand horsemen, and people as the sand which is on the sea-shore in multitude." On the other hand, Saul on his part, "blew the trumpet through all the land," and summoned all Israelites to him. They came together to him at Gilgal. And the Philistines came with their great host, and pitched over against him. Thus the two armies remained in

sight of each other, and then it was that Saul's trial
began.

Before Saul went to battle, it was necessasy to offer a
burnt sacrifice to the Lord, and to beg of Him a blessing on the arms of Israel. He could have no hope of
victory, unless this act of religious worship was performed. Now priests only and prophets were God's
ministers, and they alone could offer sacrifice. Kings
could not, unless they were specially commanded to do so
by Almighty God. Saul had no leave to offer sacrifice;
yet a sacrifice must be offered before he could fight; what
must he do? He must wait for Samuel, who had said
that he would come to him for that purpose. " Thou
shalt go down before me to Gilgal," says Samuel to
him, " and behold, I will come down unto thee, to
offer burnt offerings, and to sacrifice sacrifices of peace
offerings; seven days shalt thou tarry till I come unto
thee, and show thee what thou shalt do [1]." Saul, you
see, was told to wait seven days till Samuel came; but
meanwhile this great trial came upon him. The people
he had gathered together to fight against the Philistines
were far inferior to them in military qualities. They
were not even soldiers; they were country-people
brought together, rising against a powerful enemy, who
was used to rule, as they were used to subjection. And,
as I have already observed, they had no regular arms:
" it came to pass," says Scripture, " in the day of battle,

[1] 1 Sam. x. 8.

that there was neither sword nor spear found in the hand of any of the people that were with Saul and Jonathan." No wonder, under these circumstances, that many did not come to Saul's army at all; many hid themselves; many fled out of the country; and of those who joined him, all were in a state of alarm, and numbers began to desert. " When the men of Israel," says Scripture, " saw that they were in a strait, then the people did hide themselves in caves, and in thickets, and in rocks, and in high places, and in pits. And some of the Hebrews went over Jordan to the land of Gad and Gilead; as for Saul, he was yet in Gilgal, and all the people followed him trembling. And he tarried seven days, according to the set time that Samuel had appointed; but Samuel came not to Gilgal, and the people were scattered from him."

What a great trial this must have been! Here was a king who had been made king for the express purpose of destroying the Philistines; he is in presence of his powerful enemy; he is anxious to fulfil his commission; he fears to fail; his reputation is at stake; he has at best a most difficult task, as his soldiers are very bad ones, and are all afraid of the enemy. His only chance, humanly speaking, is to strike a blow; if he delays, he can expect nothing but total defeat; the longer he delays, the more frightened his men will become. Yet he is told to wait seven days; seven long days must he wait; he does wait through them; and to his great mortification

and despair, his soldiers begin to desert; day after day
more and more leave him : what will be the end of this?
Yet does he govern his feelings so far, as to wait all
through the seven days. So far he acquits himself well
in the trial; he was told simply to wait seven days, and
in spite of the risk, he does wait. Though he sees his
army crumbling away, and the enemy ready to attack
him, he obeys God; he obeys His prophet; he does
nothing; he looks out for Samuel's coming.

At length the seven days are gone and over; those
weary wearing days, that long trial of a week, through
every hour of which he was tempted to advance against
the enemy, yet every hour had to restrain his fierce and
impatient spirit. Now then is the time for Samuel to
come; he said he would come at the end of seven days,
and the days are ended. Now at length is the time for
Saul to be relieved. For seven days the Philistines, for
some cause or other, have not attacked him; a wonderful chance it is; he may breathe freely; every hour,
every minute he expects to hear that Samuel has joined
the camp. But now, when his trial seemed over, behold
a second trial—Samuel comes not. The prophet of God
said he would come; the prophet of God does not come
as he said.

Why Samuel did not come, we are not informed;
except that we see it was God's will to try Saul still
further; however, he did not come, and now let us
observe what was Saul's conduct.

Hitherto he had acquitted himself well; he had obeyed to the letter the command of God by His prophet. He had waited in faith though in fear; he feared the Philistines, but had faith in God. Oh that he had continued in his faith! but his faith gave way when his trial was prolonged.

When Samuel did not come, there was no one of course to offer sacrifice; what was to be done? Saul ought to have waited still longer, till Samuel did come. He had had faith in God hitherto, he should have had faith still. He had hitherto trusted that God would save him from the enemy, though his army was scattered, in God's own way. God fights not with sword and bow; He can give victory to whom He will, and when He will; "with His own right hand, and His holy arm," can He accomplish His purposes. Saul was God's servant, and therefore he might securely trust in God. He had trusted for seven days; he might go on trusting for eight, nine, or ten. And let it be observed, that this fresh trial was hardly a greater trial than before, for this reason—that his faith hitherto had met with its reward. Though the Philistines were in his front, and his own men were deserting, yet, strange to say, the Philistines had not attacked him. Thus he had had proof that God could defend him from them. He who had kept him so safely for seven days, why should He not also on the eighth? however, he did not feel this, and so he took a very rash and fatal step.

That step was as follows: since Samuel had not come, he determined to offer the burnt sacrifice instead of him; he determined to do what he could not do without a great sin; viz. intrude into a sacred office to which he was not called; nay, to do what he really could not do at all; for he might call it a sacrifice, but it would not be really such, unless a priest or prophet offered it. You know how great a crime it is for persons now to become teachers and preachers, or to baptize or administer the Lord's Supper without authority; this was Saul's crime, he determined on sacrificing, without being an appointed minister of God. This is a crime often denounced in Scripture, as in the case of Korah, and Jeroboam, and Uzziah. Korah was swallowed up by the earth on account of it; Jeroboam had his hand withered, and was punished in his family; and Uzziah was smitten with leprosy. Yet this was Saul's sin. "And Saul said," in the words of the text, "Bring hither a burnt offering to me, and peace offerings; and he offered the burnt offering." Now observe what happened immediately afterwards. "And it came to pass, that as soon as he had made an end of offering the burnt offering, behold, Samuel came, and Saul went out to meet him, that he might salute him." You see, if he had waited but one hour more, he would have been saved this sin; in other words, he would have succeeded in his trial instead of failing. But he failed, and the consequence was, he lost God's favour, and forfeited his kingdom.

Let us observe what Samuel said to him, and what he answered; "And Samuel said, What hast thou done? And Saul said, Because I saw that the people were scattered from me, and that thou camest not within the days appointed, and that the Philistines gathered themselves together to Michmash; therefore, said I, The Philistines will come down now upon me to Gilgal, and I have not made supplication unto the Lord: I forced myself, therefore, and offered a burnt offering." Such was his excuse; and now hear what Samuel thought of it: "And Samuel said to Saul, Thou hast done foolishly: thou hast not kept the commandment of the Lord thy God, which He commanded thee: for now would the Lord have established thy kingdom upon Israel for ever. But now thy kingdom shall not continue: the Lord hath sought Him a man after His own heart, and the Lord hath commanded him to be captain over His people, because thou hast not kept that which the Lord commanded thee." Such was the end of Saul's trial: he fell; he was not obedient; and in consequence he forfeited God's favour.

How much is there in this melancholy history which applies to us, my brethren, at this day, though it happened some thousand years ago! Man is the same in every age, and God Almighty is the same; and thus what happened to Saul, the king of Israel, is, alas! daily fulfilled in us, to our great shame. We all, as Saul, have been raised by God to great honour and glory; not, indeed, glory of this world, but unseen spiritual glory. We were born in sin, and the children of wrath; and He has caused us to be baptized with water and the Spirit in the Name of Father, Son, and Holy Ghost; and as Saul, by being anointed with oil by Samuel, was made king of Israel, so we, by baptism, are made kings, not kings of this world, but kings and princes in the heavenly kingdom of Christ. He is our head, and we are His brethren; He has sat down on His throne on high, and has been crowned by His Eternal Father as Lord and Christ; and we, too, by being made His brethren, partake His unseen, His heavenly glory. Though we be poor in this world, yet, when we were baptized, we, like Saul, were made strong in the Lord, powerful princes, with Angels to wait upon us, and with a place on Christ's throne in prospect. Hence, I say, we are, like Saul, favoured by God's free grace; and in consequence we are put on our trial like Saul—we are all tried in one way or another; and now consider how many there are who fall like Saul.

1. How many are there who, when in distress of any kind, in want of means, or of necessaries, forget, like Saul, that their distress, whatever it is, comes from God; that God brings it on them, and that God will remove it in His own way, if they trust in Him: but

who, instead of waiting for His time, take their own way, their own bad way, and impatiently hasten the time, and thus bring on themselves judgment! Sometimes, telling an untruth will bring them out of their difficulties, and they are tempted to do so. They make light of the sin; they say they cannot help themselves, that they are forced to it, as Saul said to Samuel; they make excuses to quiet their conscience; and instead of bearing the trial well, enduring their poverty, or whatever the trouble may be, they do not shrink from a deliberate lie, which God hears. Or, again, in like circumstances, they are tempted to steal; and they argue that they are in greater want than the person they injure, or that he will never miss what they take; and that they would not take it, were not their distress so great. Thus they act like Saul, and thus they tempt God in turn to deprive them of their heavenly inheritance. Or further, perhaps, they both steal and lie also; first steal, and then lie in order to hide their theft.

2. Again, how many are there who, when in unpleasant situations, are tempted to do what is wrong in order to get out of them, instead of patiently waiting God's time! They have, perhaps, unkind parents, and they are so uncomfortable at home, that they take the first opportunity which presents itself of getting away. They marry irreligious persons, not asking themselves the question whether they are irreligious, merely from

impatience to get out of their present discomfort; " Any thing but this," they say. What is this but to act like Saul? *he* had very little peace or quiet all the time he remained in presence of the enemy, with his own people falling away from him; and he, too, took an unlawful means to get out of his difficulty. And so, again, when persons have harsh masters and employers, or trouble-some neighbours, or are engaged in employments which they do not like, they often forget that all this is from God's providence, that to Him they must look up, that He who imposed it can take it away, can take it away in His good time, and without their sin. But they, like Saul, are impatient, and will not wait. And, again, are not some of us tempted to be impatient at the religious disadvantages we lie under; and instead of waiting for God's time, and God's prophet, take the matter into our own hand, leave the place where God has put us, and join some other communion, in order (as we hope) to have clearer light and fuller privileges?

3. Again, how many are there who, though their hearts are not right before God, yet have some sort of religiousness, and by it deceive themselves into an idea that they are religious! Observe, Saul in his way was a religious man; I say, in *his* way, but not in God's way; yet His very disobedience *he* might consider an act of religion. He offered sacrifice *rather* than go to battle without a sacrifice. An openly irreligious man would have drawn up his army and fallen upon the

Philistines without any religious service at all. Saul did not do this; no, he wished that an act of worship and prayer should precede the battle; he desired to have God's blessing upon him; and perversely, while he felt that blessing to be necessary, he did not feel that the only way of gaining it was seeking it *in the way* which God had appointed; that, whereas God had not made him His minister, he could not possibly offer the burnt offering acceptably. Thus he deceived himself; and thus many men deceive themselves now; not casting off religion altogether, but choosing their religion for themselves, as Saul did, and fancying they can be religious without being obedient.

4. Again, how many are there, who bear half the trial God puts on them, but not the whole of it; who go on well for a time, and then fall away! Saul bore on for seven days, and fainted not; on the eighth day his faith failed him. Oh may we persevere to the end! Many fall away. Let us watch and pray. Let us not get secure. Let us not think it enough to have got through one temptation well; through our whole life we are on trial. When one temptation is over, another comes; and, perhaps, our having got through one well, will be the occasion of our falling under the next, if we be not on our guard; because it may make us secure and confident, as if we had already conquered, and were safe.

5. Once more, how many are there, who, in a narrow

grudging cold-hearted way, go by the letter of God's commandments, while they neglect the spirit! Instead of considering what Christ wishes them to do, they take His words one by one, and will only accept them in their bare necessary meaning. They do not throw their hearts upon Scripture, and try to consider it as the voice of a Living and Kind Lord and Master speaking to them, but they take it to mean as little as it can. They are wanting in love. Saul was told to wait seven days—he *did* wait seven days; and then he thought he might do what he chose. He, in effect, said to Samuel, "I have done just what you told me." Yes, he fulfilled Samuel's directions literally and rigidly, but not in the spirit of love. Had he loved the Word of God, he would not have been so precise and exact in his reckoning, but would have waited still longer. And, in like manner, persons now-a-days, imitating him, too often say, when taxed with any offence, "Why is it wrong? Where is it so said in Scripture? Show us the text:" all which only shows that they obey carnally, in the letter, and not in the spirit.

How will all excuses, which sinners now make to blind and deaden their consciences, fail them in the Last Day! Saul had his excuses for disobedience. He did not confess he was wrong, but he argued; but Samuel with a word reproved, and convicted, and silenced, and sentenced him. And so in the Day of Judgment all our actions will be tried as by fire. The

All-knowing, All-holy Judge, our Saviour Jesus Christ, will sit on His throne, and with the breath of His mouth He will scatter away all idle excuses on which men now depend; and the secrets of men's hearts will be revealed. Then shall be seen who it is that serveth God, and who serveth Him not; who serve Him with the lips, who with the heart; who are hypocrites, and who are true.

God give us grace to be in the number of those whose faith and whose love is without hypocrisy or pretence; who obey out of a pure heart and a good conscience; who sincerely wish to know God's will, and who do it as far as they know it !

SERMON IV.

The Call of David.

"*So David prevailed over the Philistine with a sling and with a stone.*"
—I SAMUEL xvii. 50.

THESE words, which are taken from the chapter
which you heard read just now in the course of
the Service [1], declare the victory which David, the man
after God's own heart, gained over Goliath, who came
out of the army of the Philistines to defy the Living
God; and they declare the manner of his gaining it.
He gained it with a sling and with a stone; that is,
by means, which to man might seem weak and hopeless,
but which God Almighty blessed and prospered. Let
no one think the history of David's calling, and his
victory over Goliath, of little importance to himself;
it is indeed interesting to read for its own sake; it
raises the mind of the Christian to God, shows us His
power, and reminds us of the wonderful deliverances
with which He visits His Church in every age; but
besides all this, this history is useful to us Christians,

[1] Fifth Sunday after Trinity.

as setting before us our own calling, and our conflict with the world, the flesh, and the devil; as such I shall now briefly consider it.

David, the son of a man in humble life, and the youngest of his brethren, was chosen by Almighty God to be His special servant,—to be a prophet, a king, a psalmist; he was anointed by Samuel to be all this; and in due time he was brought forward by Almighty God, and as a first act of might, slew the heathen giant Goliath, as described in the text. Now let us apply all this to ourselves.

1. David was the son of a Bethlehemite, one among the families of Israel, with nothing apparently to recommend him to God; the youngest of his brethren, and despised by them. He was sent to feed the sheep; and his father, though doubtless he loved him dearly, yet seems to have thought little of him. For when Samuel came to Jesse at God's command, in order to choose one of his sons from the rest as God might direct him, Jesse did not bring David before him, though he did bring all his other children. Thus David seemed born to live and die among his sheep. His brothers were allowed to engage in occupations which the world thinks higher and more noble. Three of them served as soldiers in the king's army, and in consequence looked down upon David; on his asking about Goliath, one of them said to him in contempt, " With whom hast thou left those few sheep in the wilderness?" Yet God took

him from the sheepfolds to make him His servant and
His friend. Now this is fulfilled in the case of all
Christians. They are by nature poor, and mean, and
nothing worth; but God chooses them, and brings
them near unto Himself. He looks not at outward
things; He chooses and decrees according to His will,
and why He chooses these men, and passes over those,
we know not. In this country many are chosen, many
are not; and why some are chosen, others not, we cannot tell. Some men are born within the bounds of holy
Church, and are baptized with her baptism; others are
not even baptized at all. Some are born of bad parents,
irreligious parents, and have no education, or a bad one.
We, on the contrary, my brethren, are born in the
Church; we have been baptized by the Church's ministers; and why this is our blessedness, and not the
blessedness of others, we cannot tell. Here we differ
from David. He was chosen above his brethren, because
he was better than they. It is expressly said, that
when Samuel was going to choose one of his elder
brethren, God said to him, "I have refused him; for
the Lord seeth not as man seeth; for man looketh on
the outward appearance, but the Lord looketh on the
heart [1];" implying, that David's heart was in a better
state than his brother's whom Samuel would have
chosen. But this is not our case; we are in nowise
better by nature than they whom God does not choose.

[1] 1 Sam. xvi. 7.

You will find good and worthy men, benevolent, charitable, upright men, among those who have never been baptized. God hath chosen all of us to salvation, not for our righteousness, but for His great mercies. He has brought us to worship Him in sacred places where His saints have worshipped for many hundred years. He has given us the aid of His ministers, and His Sacraments, and His Holy Scriptures, and the Ancient Creed. To others, Scripture is a sealed book, though they hold it in their hands; but to us it is in good measure an open book, through God's mercy, if we but use our advantages, if we have but spiritual eyes and ears, to read and hear it faithfully. To others, the Sacraments and other rites are but dead ordinances, carnal ceremonies, which profit not, like those of the Jewish Law, outward forms, beggarly elements, as they themselves often confess; but to us, if we have faith, they are full of grace and power. Thus all we have been chosen by God's grace unto salvation, in a special way, in which many others around us have not been chosen, as God passed over David's seven brethren, and chose him.

2. Observe, too, God chose him, whose occupation was that of a shepherd; for He chooses not the great men of the world. He passes by the rich and noble; He chooses "the poor, rich in faith, and heirs of the kingdom which He hath promised to them that love Him[1]," as St. James says. David was a shepherd.

---

[1] James ii. 5.

The Angel appeared to the shepherds as they kept watch over their sheep at night. The most solitary, the most unlearned, God hears, God looks upon, God visits, God blesses, God brings to glory, if he is but "rich in faith." Many of you are not great in this world, my brethren, many of you are poor; but the greatest king upon earth, even Solomon in all his glory, might well exchange places with you, if you are God's children; for then you are greater than the greatest of kings. Our Saviour said, that even the lilies of the field were more gloriously arrayed than Solomon; for the lily is a living thing, the work of God; and all the glories of a king, his purple robe, and his jewelled crown, all this is but the dead work of man; and the lowest and humblest work of God is far better and more glorious than the highest work of man. But if this be true, even of God's lower works, what shall be said of His higher? If even the lilies of the field, which are cut down and cast into the oven, are more glorious than this world's greatest glory, what shall be said of God's nobler works in the soul of man? what shall be said of the dispensation of the Spirit which "exceeds in glory?" of that new creation of the soul, whereby He makes us His children, who by birth were children of Adam, and slaves of the devil, gives us a new and heavenly nature, implants His Holy Spirit within us, and washes away all our sins? This is the portion of the Christian, high or low: and all glories

of this world fade away before it; king and subject,
man of war and keeper of sheep, are all on a level in
the kingdom of Christ; for they one and all receive
those far exceeding and eternal blessings, which make
this world's distinctions, though they remain distinctions just as before, yet so little, so unimportant, in
comparison of the "glory that excelleth," that it is
not worth while thinking about them. One person is
a king and rules, another is a subject and obeys; but
if both are Christians, both have in common a gift so
great, that in the sight of it, the difference between
ruling and obeying is as nothing. All Christians are
kings in God's sight; they are kings in His unseen
kingdom, in His spiritual world, in the Communion
of Saints. They seem like other men, but they have
crowns on their heads, and glorious robes around them,
and Angels to wait on them, though our bodily eyes
see it not. Such are all Christians, high and low; all
Christians who remain in that state in which Holy
Baptism placed them. Baptism placed you in this
blessed state. God did not wait till you should do some
good thing before He blessed you. No! He knew you
could do no good thing of yourselves. So He came to
you first; He loved you before you loved Him; He
gave you a work which He first made you able to do.
He placed you in a new and heavenly state, in which,
while you remain, you are safe. He said not to you,
"Obey Me, and I will give you a kingdom;" but "Lo

I give you a kingdom freely and first of all; now obey Me henceforth, for you can, and you shall remain in it;" not "Obey Me, and I will then give you the Holy Spirit as a reward;" but "I give you that great gift in order that you may obey Me." He first gives, and then commands; He tells us to obey Him, not to gain His favour, but in order not to lose it. We are by nature diseased and helpless. We cannot please Him; we cannot move hand or foot; He says not to us, "Get well first, and I will receive you;" but He begins a cure in us, and receives us, and then says, "Take care not to go back; take care of yourselves; beware of a relapse; keep out of danger." Such then is your state, my brethren, unless you have fallen from Christ. If you are living in His faith and fear, you are kings— kings in God's unseen and spiritual kingdom; and that, though like David, you are but keeping sheep, or driving cattle, or, again, working with your hands, or serving in a family, or at any other lowly labour. God seeth not as man seeth, He hath chosen you.

3. Next, observe God chose David by means of the Prophet Samuel. He did not think it enough to choose him silently, but He called him by a voice. And, in like manner, when God calls us, He does so openly; He sent His minister, the Prophet Samuel, to David, and He sends His ministers to us. He said to Samuel, "Fill thy horn with oil, and go, and I will send thee to Jesse the Bethlehemite; for I have provided Me a

king among his sons." God was looking out for a king, and sent Samuel to David. And so, in like manner, God is looking out now for kings to fill thrones in His Son's eternal kingdom, and to sit at His right hand and His left; and He sends His ministers to those whom He hath from eternity chosen. He does not say to them, "Fill thy horn with oil," but "Fill thy font with water;" for as He chose David by pouring oil upon his head, so does He choose us by Baptism. So far, then, God chooses now as He did then, by an outward sign. Samuel was told to do then, what Christ's ministers are told to do now. The one chose David by means of oil, and the other choose Christians by means of water. In this, however, there is a difference. Samuel could choose but one. He was not allowed to choose more than one; him, namely, whom God pointed out; but now Christ's ministers (blessed be His name!) may choose and baptize all whom they meet with; there is no restriction, no narrowness; they need not wait to be told whom to choose. Christ says, "Compel them to come in." Again, the Prophet says, "Ho, every one that thirsteth, come ye to the waters." Now every one by nature thirsteth; every soul born into the world is in a spiritual sickness, in a wasting fever of mind; he has no rest, no ease, no peace, no true happiness. Till he is made partaker of Christ he is hopeless and miserable. Christ then, in His mercy, having died for all, gives His ministers leave to apply

His saving death to all whom they can find. Not one or two, but thousands upon thousands are gifted with His high blessings. "Samuel took the horn of oil, and anointed" David "in the midst of his brethren." And so Christ's ministers take water, and baptize; yet not merely one out of a family, but all; for God's mercies are poured as wide as the sun's light in the heavens, they enlighten all they fall upon.

4. When Samuel had anointed David, observe what followed. "Samuel took the horn of oil, and anointed him in the midst of his brethren; and the Spirit of the Lord came upon David from that day forward." And so, also, when Christ's ministers baptize, the Spirit of the Lord comes upon the child baptized henceforth; nay, dwells in him, for the Christian's gift is far greater even than David's. God's Spirit did but come upon David, and visit him from time to time; but He vouchsafes to dwell within the Christian, so as to make his heart and body His temple. Now what was there in the oil, which Samuel used, to produce so great an effect? nothing at all. Oil has no power in itself; but God gave it a power. In like manner the Prophet Elisha told Naaman the Syrian to bathe in Jordan, and so he was healed of his leprosy. Naaman said, What is Jordan more than other rivers? how can Jordan heal? It could not heal, except that God's power made it heal. Did not our Saviour feed five thousand persons with a few loaves and fishes? how could that be? by His

power. How could water become wine? by His power. And so now, that same Divine power, which made water wine, multiplied the bread, gave water power to heal an incurable disease, and made oil the means of gifting David with the Holy Spirit, that power now also makes the water of Baptism a means of grace and glory. The water is like other water; we see no difference by the eye; we use it, we throw it away; but God is with it. God is with it, as with the oil which Samuel took with him. Water is something more than water in its effects in the hand of Christ's Minister, with the words of grace; it does, what by nature it cannot do; it is heavenly water, not earthly.

5. Further, I would have you observe this. Though David received the gift of God's Holy Spirit, yet nothing came of it all at once. He still seemed like any other man. He went back to the sheep. Then Saul sent for him to play to him on the harp; and then he went back to the sheep again. Except that he had strength given him to kill a lion and a bear which came against his flock, he did no great thing. The Spirit of the Lord had come upon him, yet it did not at once make him a prophet or a king. All was to come in good time, not at once. So it is with Christian Baptism. Nothing shows, for some time, that the Spirit of God is come into, and dwells in the child baptized; it looks like any other child, it is pained, it frets, is weak, is wayward, like any other child; for

"the Lord seeth not as man seeth; for man looketh at the outward appearance, but the Lord looketh on the heart." And "He who seeth the heart," seeth in the child the presence of the Spirit, "the mind of the Spirit" "which maketh intercession for the Saints." God the Holy Ghost leads on the heirs of grace marvellously. You recollect when our Saviour was baptized, "immediately the Spirit of God led Him into the wilderness." What happened one way in our Saviour's course, happens in ours also. Sooner or later that work of God is manifested, which was at first secret. David went up to see his brothers, who were in the battle; he had no idea that he was going to fight the giant Goliath; and so it is now, children are baptized before they know what is to happen to them. They sport and play as if there was no sorrow in the world, and no high destinies upon themselves; they are heirs of the kingdom without knowing it; but God is with those whom He has chosen, and in His own time and way He fashions His Saints for His everlasting kingdom: in His own perfect and adorable counsels He brings them forward to fight with Goliath.

6. And now, let us inquire who is our Goliath? who is it we have to contend with? The answer is plain; the devil is our Goliath: we have to fight Satan, who is far more fearful and powerful than ten thousand giants, and who would to a certainty destroy us were not God with us; but praised be His Name, He is

with us. "Greater is He that is with us, than he that is in the world." David was first anointed with God's Holy Spirit, and then, after a while, brought forward to fight Goliath. We too are first baptized, and then brought forward to fight the devil. We are not brought to fight him at once; for some years we are almost without a fight, when we are infants. By degrees our work comes upon us; as children we have to fight with him a little; as time goes on, the fight opens; and at length we have our great enemy marching against us with sword and spear, as Goliath came against David. And when this war has once begun, it lasts through life.

7. What then ought you to do, my brethren, when thus assailed? How must you behave when the devil comes against you? he has many ways of attack; sometimes he comes openly, sometimes craftily, sometimes he tempts you, sometimes he frightens you, but whether he comes in a pleasing or a frightful form, be sure, if you saw him himself with your eyes, he would always be hateful, monstrous, and abominable. Therefore he keeps himself out of sight. But be sure he is all this; and, as believing it, take the whole armour of God, that you may be able to stand in the evil day, and having done all, to stand. Quit you like men, be strong. Be like David, very courageous to do God's will. Think what would have happened had David played the coward, and refused to obey God's inward voice stirring him up to fight

Goliath. He would have lost his calling, he would have been tried, and have failed. The Prophet's oil would have profited him nothing, or rather would have increased his condemnation. The Spirit of God would have departed from him as He departed from Saul, who also had been anointed. So, also, our privileges will but increase our future punishment, unless we use them. *He* is truly and really born of God in whom the Divine seed takes root; others are regenerated to their condemnation. Despise not the gift that is in you : despise not the blessing which by God's free grace you have, and others have not. There is nothing to boast in, that you are God's people; rather the thought is an anxious one; you have much more to answer for.

When, then, Satan comes against you, recollect you are already dedicated, made over, to God ; you are God's property, you have no part with Satan and his works, you are servants to another, you are espoused to Christ. When Satan comes against you, fear not, waver not; but pray to God, and He will help you. Say to Satan with David, "Thou comest against me with a sword, and with a spear, and with a shield; but I come to thee in the name of the Lord of Hosts." Thou comest to me with temptation; thou wouldest allure me with the pleasures of sin for a season; thou wouldest kill me, nay, thou wouldest make me kill myself with sinful thoughts, words, and deeds; thou wouldest make me a self-murderer, tempting me by evil companions, and light conversation, and pleasant sights, and strong stirrings of heart; thou wouldest make me profane the Lord's day by riot; thou wouldest keep me from Church; thou wouldest make my thoughts rove when they should not; thou wouldest tempt me to drink, and to curse, and to swear, and to jest, and to lie, and to steal: but I know thee; thou art Satan, and I come unto thee in the name of the Living God, in the Name of Jesus Christ my Saviour. That is a powerful name, which can put to flight many foes: Jesus is a name at which devils tremble. To speak it, is to scare away many a bad thought. I come against thee in His All-powerful, All-conquering Name. David came on with a staff; my staff is the Cross—the Holy Cross on which Christ suffered, in which I glory, which is my salvation. David chose five smooth stones out of the brook, and with them he smote the giant. We, too, have armour, not of this world, but of God; weapons which the world despises, but which are powerful in God. David took not sword, spear, or shield; but he slew Goliath with a sling and a stone. Our weapons are as simple, as powerful. The Lord's Prayer is one such weapon; when we are tempted to sin, let us turn away, kneel down seriously and solemnly, and say to God that prayer which the Lord taught us. The Creed is another weapon, equally powerful, through God's grace, equally contemptible in the eyes of the world. One or two holy texts, such as our Saviour used when He was tempted by the devil, is another weapon for our need. The Sacrament of the Lord's Supper is another such, and greater; holy, mysterious, life-giving, but equally simple. What is so simple as a little bread and a little wine? but, in the hands of the Spirit of God, it is the power of God unto salvation. God grant us grace to use the arms which He gives us; not to neglect them, not to take arms of our own! God grant us to use His arms, and to conquer!

SERMON V.

Curiosity a Temptation to Sin.

" Enter not into the path of the wicked, and go not in the way of evil men. Avoid it, pass not by it, turn from it, and pass away."—PROVERBS iv. 14, 15.

ONE chief cause of the wickedness which is every where seen in the world, and in which, alas! each of us has more or less his share, is our curiosity to have some fellowship with darkness, some experience of sin, to know what the pleasures of sin are like. I believe it is even thought unmanly by many persons (though they may not like to say so in plain words), unmanly and a thing to be ashamed of, to have no knowledge of sin by experience, as if it argued a strange seclusion from the world, a childish ignorance of life, a simpleness and narrowness of mind, and a superstitious, slavish fear. Not to know sin by experience brings upon a man the laughter and jests of his companions: nor is it wonderful this should be the case in the descendants of that guilty pair to whom Satan in the beginning held out admittance into a strange world of knowledge and enjoyment, as the reward of disobedience to God's commandment. "When the woman saw that the tree was good for food, and that it was pleasant to the eyes, and a tree to be desired to make one wise, she took of the fruit thereof, and did eat, and gave also unto her husband with her, and he did eat [1]." A discontent with the abundance of blessings which were given, because something was withheld, was the sin of our first parents: in like manner, a wanton roving after things forbidden, a curiosity to know what it was to be as the heathen, was one chief source of the idolatries of the Jews; and we at this day inherit with them a like nature from Adam.

I say, curiosity strangely moves us to disobedience, in order that we may have experience of the pleasure of disobedience. Thus we "rejoice in our youth, and let our heart cheer us in the days of our youth, and walk in the ways of our heart, and in the sight of our eyes [2]." And we thus intrude into things forbidden, in various ways; in reading what we should not read, in hearing what we should not hear, in seeing what we should not see, in going into company whither we should not go, in presumptuous reasonings and arguings when we should have faith, in acting as if we were our own masters where we should obey. We indulge our reason, we indulge our passions, we indulge our ambition, our vanity, our love of power; we throw ourselves into the

[1] Gen. iii. 6.   [2] Eccles. xi. 9.

society of bad, worldly, or careless men; and all the
while we think that, after having acquired this miserable knowledge of good and evil, we can return to our
duty, and continue where we left off; merely going
aside a moment to shake ourselves, as Samson did, and
with an ignorance like his, that our true heavenly
strength is departed from us.

Now this delusion arises from Satan's craft, the father
of lies, who knows well that if he can get us once to sin,
he can easily make us sin twice and thrice, till at length
we are taken captive at his will[1]. He sees that curiosity is man's great and first snare, as it was in paradise; and he knows that, if he can but force a way into
his heart by this chief and exciting temptation, those
temptations of other kinds, which follow in life, will
easily prevail over us; and, on the other hand, that if
we resist the beginnings of sin, there is every prospect
through God's grace that we shall continue in a religious way. His plan of action then lies plain before
him—to tempt us violently, while the world is new to
us, and our hopes and feelings are eager and restless.
Hence is seen the Divine wisdom, as well as the merciful
consideration, of the advice contained in so many parts
of Scripture, as in the text, " Enter not into the path
of the wicked, and go not into the way of evil men.
Avoid it, pass not by it, turn from it, and pass away."

Let us, then, now for a few moments give our minds

[1] 2 Tim. ii. 26.

F

to the consideration of this plain truth, which we have heard so often that for that very reason we are not unlikely to forget it—that the great thing in religion is to set off well; to resist the beginnings of sin, to flee temptation, to avoid the company of the wicked. " Enter not into the path of the wicked . . . . avoid it, pass not by it, turn from it, pass away."

1. And for this reason, first of all, because it is hardly possible to delay our flight without rendering flight impossible. When I say, resist the beginnings of evil, I do not mean the first act merely, but the rising thought of evil. Whatever the temptation may be, there may be no time to wait and gaze, without being caught. Woe to us if Satan (so to say) sees us first; for, as in the case of some beast of prey, for him to see us is to master us. Directly we are made aware of the temptation, we shall, if we are wise, turn our backs upon it, without waiting to think and reason about it; we shall engage our mind in other thoughts. There are temptations when this advice is especially necessary; but under all it is highly seasonable.

2. For consider, in the next place, what must in all cases be the consequence of allowing evil thoughts to be present to us, though we do not actually admit them into our hearts. This, namely,—we shall make ourselves familiar with them. Now our great security against sin lies in being shocked at it. Eve gazed and reflected when she should have fled. It is sometimes said

"Second thoughts are best:" this is true in many cases; but there are times when it is very false, and when, on the contrary, first thoughts are best. For sin is like the serpent, which seduced our first parents. We know that some serpents have the power of what is called "fascinating." Their eye has the power of subduing—nay, in a strange way, of alluring—their victim, who is reduced to utter helplessness, cannot flee away, nay, rather is obliged to approach, and (as it were) deliver himself up to them; till in their own time they seize and devour him. What a dreadful figure this is of the power of sin and the devil over our hearts! At first our conscience tells us, in a plain straightforward way, what is right and what is wrong; but when we trifle with this warning, our reason becomes perverted, and comes in aid of our wishes, and deceives us to our ruin. Then we begin to find, that there are arguments available in behalf of bad deeds, and we listen to these till we come to think them true; and then, if perchance better thoughts return, and we make some feeble effort to get at the truth really and sincerely, we find our minds by that time so bewildered that we do not know right from wrong.

Thus, for instance, every one is shocked at cursing and swearing when he first hears it; and at first he cannot help even showing that he is shocked; that is, he looks grave and downcast, and feels uncomfortable. But when he has once got accustomed to such profane talking, and been laughed out of his strictness, and has begun to think it manly, and has been persuaded to join in it, then he soon learns to defend it. He says he means no harm by it; that it does no one any harm; that it is only so many words, and that every body uses them. Here is an instance in which disobedience to what we know to be right makes us blind.

Again, this same confusion frequently happens in the case of temptations from the world. We fear worldly loss or discredit; or we hope some advantage; and we feel tempted to act so as to secure, at any rate, the worldly good, or to avoid the evil. Now in all such cases of conduct there is no end of arguing about right or wrong, if we once begin; there are numberless ways of acting, each of which may be speciously defended by argument, but plain, pure-hearted common sense, generally speaking, at the very first sight decides the question for us without argument; but if we do not listen promptly to this secret monitor, its light goes out at once, and we are left to the mercy of mere conjecture, and grope about with but second-best guides. Then seeming arguments in favour of deceit and evil compliance with the world's wishes, or of disgraceful indolence, urge us, and either prevail, or at least so confuse us, that we do not know how to act. Alas! in ancient days it happened in this way, that Christians who were brought before their heathen persecutors for punishment, because they were Christians, sometimes came short of the crown of martyrdom, " having loved this present world [1]," and so lost their way in the mazes of Satan's crafty arguments.

Temptations to unbelief may also be mentioned here. Speculating wantonly on sacred subjects, and jesting about them, offend us at first; and we turn away: but if in an evil hour we are seduced by the cleverness or wit of a writer or speaker, to listen to his impieties, who can say where we shall stop? Can we save ourselves from the infection of his profaneness? we cannot hope to do so. And when we come to a better mind (if by God's grace this be afterwards granted to us), what will be our state? like the state of men who have undergone some dreadful illness, which changes the constitution of the body. That ready and clear perception of right and wrong, which before directed us, will have disappeared, as beauty of person, or keenness of eye-sight in bodily disorders; and when we begin to try to make up our minds which way lies the course of duty on particular trials, we shall bring enfeebled, unsteady powers to the examination; and when we move to act, our limbs (as it were) will move the contrary way, and we shall do wrong when we wish to do right.

3. But there is another wretched effect of sinning once, which sometimes takes place;—not only the sinning that once itself, but being so seduced by it. as forthwith to continue in the commission of it ever

[1] 2 Tim. iv. 10.

afterwards, without seeking for arguments to meet our conscience withal; from a mere brutish, headstrong, infatuate greediness after its bad pleasures. There are beasts of prey which are said to abstain from blood till they taste it, but once tasting it, ever seek it: and, in like manner, there is a sort of thirst for sin which is born with us, but which grace quenches, and which is thus kept under *till* we, by our own act, rouse it again; and which, when once aroused, never can be allayed. We sin, while we confess the wages of sin to be death.

4. Sometimes, I say, this is the immediate effect of a first transgression; and if not the immediate effect, yet it is always the tendency and the end of sinning at length, viz. to enslave us to it. Temptation is very powerful, it is true, when it comes first; but, then, its power lies in its own novelty; and, on the other hand, there is power in the heart itself, divinely given, to resist it; but when we have long indulged sin, the mind has become sinful in its habit and character, and the Spirit of God having departed, it has no principle within it of strength sufficient to save it from spiritual death. What being can change its own nature? that would be almost ceasing to be itself: fire cannot cease to burn; the leopard changes not its spots, and ceases not to rend and devour; and the soul which has often sinned, cannot help sinning; but in this respect awfully differing from the condition of the senseless elements or brute animals,—that its present state is all its own fault; that it might

have hindered it, and will have one day to answer for not having hindered it.

Thus, easy as it is to avoid sin first of all, at length it is (humanly speaking) impossible. "Enter not into its path," saith the wise man; the two paths of right and wrong start from the same point, and at first are separated by a very small difference, so easy (comparatively) is it to choose the right instead of the wrong way: but wait awhile, and pursue the road leading to destruction, and you will find the distance between the two has widened beyond measurement, and that between them a great gulf has been sunk, so that you cannot pass from the one to the other, though you desire it ever so earnestly [1].

Now to what do considerations such as these lead us, but to our Lord's simple and comprehensive precept, which is the same as Solomon's, but more impressively and solemnly urged on us by the manner and time of His giving it? "Watch and pray, lest ye enter into temptation." To enter not the path of the wicked, to avoid it, and pass by it, what is this but the exercise of *watching?* Therefore He insists upon it so much, knowing that in it our safety lies. But now, on the other hand, consider *how* many are there among us who can be said to watch and pray? Is not the utmost we do to offer on Sunday some kind of prayer in Church to God; or sometimes some short prayer morning and

[1] Luke xvi. 26.

evening in the week; and then go into the world with
the same incaution and forgetfulness as if we had never
entertained a serious thought? We go through the
business of the day, quite forgetting, to any practical
purpose, that all business has snares in it, and therefore
needs caution. Let us ask ourselves this question,
"How often do we think of Satan in the course of the
day as our great tempter?" Yet surely he does not
cease to be active because we do not think of him; and
surely, too, his powers and devices were revealed to us
by Almighty God for the very purpose, that being
not ignorant of them, we might watch against them.
Who among us will not confess, that many is the time
that he has mixed with the world, forgetting who
the god of this world is? or rather, are not a great
many of us living in habitual forgetfulness that this
world is a scene of trial; that is, that this is its *chief*
character, that all its employments, its pleasures, its
occurrences, even the most innocent, the most acceptable
to God, and the most truly profitable in themselves,
are all the while so handled by Satan as may be the
most conducive to our ruin, if he can possibly contrive
it? There is nothing gloomy or superstitious in this,
as the plain words of Scripture will abundantly prove
to every inquirer. We are told "that the devil, our
adversary, as a roaring lion walketh about, seeking
whom he may devour[1];" and therefore are warned to

[1] 1 Pet. v. 8.

" be sober, be vigilant." And assuredly our true comfort lies, not in disguising the truth from ourselves, but in knowing something more than this;—that though Satan is against us, God is for us; that greater is He that is in us, than he that is in the world[1]; and that He in every temptation will make a way for us to escape, that we may be able to bear it[2].

God does His part most surely; and Satan too does his part: we alone are unconcerned. Heaven and hell are at war for us and against us, yet we trifle, and let life go on at random. Heaven and hell are before us as our own future abode, one or other of them; yet our own interest moves us no more than God's mercy. We treat sin, not as an enemy to be feared, abhorred, and shunned, but as a misfortune and a weakness; we do not pity and shun sinful men, but we enter into their path so far as to keep company with them; and next, being tempted to copy them, we fall almost without an effort.

Be not you thus deceived and overcome, my brethren, by an evil heart of unbelief. Make up your minds to take God for your portion, and pray to Him for grace to enable you so to do. Avoid the great evils of leisure, avoid the snare of having time on your hands. Avoid all bad thoughts, all corrupt or irreligious books, avoid all bad company : let nothing seduce you into it. Though you may be laughed at for your strictness; though you may lose thereby amusements which you

---

[1] 1 John iv. 4.   [2] 1 Cor. x. 13.

would like to partake of; though you may thereby be ignorant of much which others know, and may appear to disadvantage when they are talking together; though you appear behind the rest of the world; though you be called a coward, or a child, or narrow-minded, or superstitious; whatever insulting words be applied to you, fear not, falter not, fail not; stand firm, quit you like men; be strong. They think that in the devil's service there are secrets worthy our inquiry, which you share not: yes, there are secrets, and such that it is a shame even to speak of them; and in like manner you have a secret which they have not, and which far surpasses theirs. "The secret of the Lord is with them that fear Him." Those who obey God and follow Christ have secret gains, so great, that, as well might we say heaven were like hell, as that these are like the gain which sinners have. They have a secret gift given them by their Lord and Saviour in proportion to their faith and love. They cannot describe it to others; they have not possession of it all at once; they cannot have the enjoyment of it at this or that time when they will. It comes and goes according to the will of the Giver. It is given but in small measure to those who begin God's service. It is not given at all to those who follow Him with a divided heart. To those who love the world, and yet are in a certain sense religious, and are well contented with such a religious state, to them it is not given. But those who give themselves up to

their Lord and Saviour, those who surrender themselves soul and body, those who honestly say, "I am
Thine, new-make me, do with me what Thou wilt," who
say so not once or twice merely, or in a transport, but
calmly and habitually; these are they who gain the
Lord's secret gift, even the "white stone, and in the
stone a new name written which no man knoweth,
saving he that receiveth it[1]." Sinners think that they
know all that religion has to give, and over and above
that, they know the pleasures of sin too. No, they do
not, cannot, never will know the secret gift of God, till
they repent and amend. They never will know what it
is to see God, till they obey; nay, though they are to
see Him at the last day, even that will be no true sight
of Him, for the sight of that Holy One will then impart
no comfort, no joy to them. They never will know the
blessedness which He has to give. They do know the
satisfaction of sinning, such as it is; and, alas! if they
go on as they are going, they will know not only what
sin is, but what hell is. But they never will know that
great secret which is hid in the Father and in the Son.

Let us not then be seduced by the Tempter and his
promises. He can show us no good. He has no good
to give us. Rather let us listen to the gracious words
of our Maker and Redeemer, "Call unto Me, and I
will answer thee, and show thee great and mighty
things, which thou knowest not[2]."

[1] Rev. ii. 17.   [2] Jer. xxxiii. 3

SERMON VI.

Miracles no Remedy for Unbelief.

*"And the Lord said unto Moses, How long will this people provoke Me?
and how long will it be ere they believe Me, for all the signs which I
have showed among them?"*—NUMBERS xiv. 11.

NOTHING, I suppose, is more surprising to us at
first reading, than the history of God's chosen
people; nay, on second and third reading, and on every
reading, till we learn to view it as God views it. It
seems strange, indeed, to most persons, that the Israelites
should have acted as they did, age after age, in spite
of the miracles which were vouchsafed to them. The
laws of nature were suspended again and again before
their eyes; the most marvellous signs were wrought
at the word of God's prophets, and for their deliverance;
yet they did not obey their great Benefactor at all
better than men now-a-days who have not these advantages, as we commonly consider them. Age after age
God visited them by Angels, by inspired messengers;
age after age they sinned. At last He sent His well-

beloved Son; and He wrought miracles before them
still more abundant, wonderful, and beneficent than any
before Him. What was the effect upon them of His
coming? St. John tells us, "Then gathered the Chief
Priests and the Pharisees a council, and said, What do
we? for this Man doeth many miracles. . . . . Then
from that day forth they took counsel together for to
put Him to death[1]."

In matter of fact, then, whatever be the reason,
nothing is gained by miracles, nothing comes of miracles, as regards our religious views, principles, and habits.
Hard as it is to believe, miracles certainly do not make
men better; the history of Israel proves it. And the
only mode of escaping this conclusion, to which some
persons feel a great repugnance, is to fancy that the
Israelites were much worse than other nations, which
accordingly has been maintained. It has often been
said, that they were stiff-necked and hard-hearted beyond
the rest of the world. Now, even supposing, for argument's sake, I should grant that they were so, this would
not sufficiently account for the strange circumstance
under consideration; for this people was not moved
at all. It is not a question of more or less: surely they
must have been altogether distinct from other men,
destitute of the feelings and opinions of other men,
nay, hardly partakers of human nature, if other men
would, as a matter of course, have been moved by those

[1] John xi. 47. 53.

miracles which had no influence whatever upon them. That there *are*, indeed, men in the world who would have been moved, and would have obeyed in consequence, I do not deny; such were to be found among the Israelites also; but I am speaking of men in general; and I say, that if the Israelites had a common nature with us, surely that insensibility which they exhibited on the whole, must be just what we should exhibit on the whole under the same circumstances.

It confirms this view of the subject to observe, that the children of Israel *are* like other men in all points of their conduct, save this insensibility, which other men have not had the opportunity to show as they had. There is no difference between their conduct and ours in point of *fact;* the difference is entirely in the external discipline to which God subjected them. Whether or not miracles ought to have influenced them in a way in which God's dealings in Providence do not influence us, so far is clear, that looking into their modes of living and of thought, we find a nature just like our own, not better indeed, but in no respect worse. Those evil tempers which the people displayed in the desert, their greediness, selfishness, murmuring, caprice, waywardness, fickleness, ingratitude, jealousy, suspiciousness, obstinacy, unbelief, all these are seen in the uneducated multitude now-a-days, according to its opportunity of displaying them.

The pride of Dathan and the presumption of Korah are still instanced in our higher ranks and among educated persons. Saul, Ahithophel, Joab, and Absalom, have had their parallels all over the world. I say there is nothing unlike the rest of mankind in the character or conduct of the chosen people; the difference solely is in God's dealings with them. They *act* as other men; it is their religion which is not as other men; it is miraculous; and the question is, how it comes to pass, their religion being different, their conduct is the same? and there are two ways of answering it; either by saying that they were worse than other men, and were not influenced by miracles when others would have been influenced (as many persons are apt to think), or (what I conceive to be the true reason) that, after all, the difference between miracle and no miracle is not so great in any case, in the case of any people, as to secure the success or account for the failure of religious truth. It was not that the Israelites were much more hard-hearted than other people, but that a miraculous religion is not much more influential than other religions.

For I repeat, though it be granted that the Israelites were much worse than others, still that will not account for the fact that miracles made no impression whatever upon them. However sensual and obstinate they may be supposed to have been in natural character, yet if it be true that a miracle has a necessary effect upon the human mind, it must be considered to have had some effect on their conduct for good or bad; if it had not a good effect, at least it must have had a bad;

whereas their miracles left them very much the same in outward appearance as men are now-a-days, who neglect such warnings as are now sent them, neither much more lawless and corrupt than they, nor the reverse. The point is, that while they were so hardened, as it appears to us, in their conduct towards their Lord and Governor, they were not much worse than other men in social life and personal behaviour. It is a rule that if men are extravagantly irreligious, profane, blasphemous, infidel, they are equally excessive and monstrous in other respects; whereas the Jews were like the Eastern nations around them, with this one peculiarity, that they had rejected direct and clear miraculous evidence, and the others had not. It seems, then, I say, to follow, that, guilty as were the Jews in disobeying Almighty God, and blind as they became from shutting their eyes to the light, they were not much more guilty than others may be in disobeying Him; that it is almost as great a sin to reject His service in the case of those who do not see miracles, as in the case of those who do; that the sight of miracles is not the way in which men come to believe and obey, nor the absence of them an excuse for not believing and obeying.

Now let me say something in explanation of this, at first sight, startling truth, that miracles on the whole would not make men in general more obedient or holy than they are, though they were generally displayed. It has sometimes been said by unbelievers, " If the

Gospel were written on the Sun, I would believe it."
Unbelievers have said so by way of excusing themselves
for not believing it, as it actually comes to them; and I
dare say some of us, my brethren, have before now
uttered the same sentiment in our hearts, either in
moments of temptation, or when under the upbraidings
of conscience for sin committed. Now let us consider,
why do we think so?

I ask, why should the sight of a miracle make you
better than you are? Do you doubt at all the being
and power of God? No. Do you doubt what you
ought to *do?* No. Do you doubt at all that the rain,
for instance, and sunshine, come from Him? or that the
fresh life of each year, as it comes, is His work, and that
all nature bursts into beauty and richness at His bidding? You do not doubt it at all. Nor do you doubt,
on the other hand, that it is your duty to obey Him
who made the world and who made you. And yet,
with the knowledge of all this, you find you cannot
prevail upon yourselves to do what you know you
should do. Knowledge is not what you want to make
you obedient. You have knowledge enough already.
Now what truth would a miracle convey to you which
you do not learn from the works of God around you?
What would it teach you concerning God which you do
not already believe without having seen it?

But, you will say, a miracle would startle you; true:
but would not the startling pass away? could you be

[VIII]   G

startled for ever ?   And what sort of a religion is that
which consists in a state of fright and disturbance ?
Are you not continually startled by the accidents of
life ?   You see, you hear things suddenly, which bring
before your minds the thoughts of God and judgment ;
calamities befall you which for the time sober you.
Startling is not conversion, any more than knowledge
is practice.

But you urge, that perhaps that startling might issue
in amendment of life ; that it might be the beginning
of a new course, though it passed away itself ; that
a miracle would not indeed convert you, but it would
be the first step towards thorough conversion ; that it
would be the turning point in your life, and would suddenly force your path into the right direction, and that in
this way shocks and startlings, and all the agitation
of the passions and affections, are really the means of
conversion, though conversion be something more than
they.   This is very true : sudden emotions—fear, hope,
gratitude, and the like, all do produce such effects sometimes ; but why is a miracle necessary to produce such
effects ?   Other things startle us besides miracles : we
have a number of accidents sent us by God to startle
us.   He has not left us without warnings, though He
has not given us miracles ; and if we are not moved and
converted by those which come upon us, the probability
is, that, like the Jews, we should not be converted by
miracles.

Yes, you say; but if one came from the dead, if you saw the spirit of some departed friend you knew on earth: what then? What would it tell you that you do not know now? Do you now in your sober reason doubt the reality of the unseen world? not at all; only you cannot get yourself to act as if it *were* real. Would such a sight produce this effect? you think it would. Now I will grant this on one supposition. Do the startling accidents which happen to you now, produce *any* lasting effect upon you? Do they lead you to *any habits* of religion? If they do produce some effect, then I will grant to you that such a strange visitation, as you have supposed, would produce a greater effect; but if the events of life which now happen to you produce *no* lasting effect on you, and this I fear is the case, then too sure I am, that a miracle too would produce no lasting effect on you, though of course it would startle you more at the time. I say, I fear that what happens to you, as it is, produces no lasting effect on you. 1 mean, that the warnings which you really have, do not bring you to any habitual and regular religiousness; they may make you a little more afraid of this or that sin, or of this or that particular indulgence of it; but they do not tend at all to make you break with the world, and convert you to God. If they did make you take up religion in earnest, though in ever so poor a way, then I will grant that miracles would make you *more* in earnest. If God's *ordinary* warnings moved you, His extraordinary would move you more. It is quite true, that a serious mind would be made more serious by seeing a miracle, but this gives no ground for saying, that minds which are *not* serious, careless, worldly, self-indulgent persons, who are made not at all better by the warnings which *are* given them, would be made serious by those miraculous warnings which are not given.

Of course it might so happen in this or that particular case,—just as the same person is moved by one warning, not by another; not moved by a warning to-day, moved by a warning to-morrow; but I am sure, taking men as we find them, miracles would leave them, as far as their conduct is concerned, very much as they are. They would be very much startled and impressed at first, but the impression would wear away. And thus our Saviour's words would come true of all those multitudes who have the Bible to read, and know what they ought to do, but do it not:—"If they hear not Moses and the Prophets," He says, "neither will they be persuaded though one rose from the dead." Do we never recollect times when we have said, "We shall never forget this; it will be a warning all through our lives"? have we never implored God's forgiveness with the most eager promises of amendment? have we never felt as if we were brought quite into a new world, in gratitude and joy? Yet was the result what we had expected? We cannot anticipate more from miracles, than before now we have anticipated from warnings, which came to nought.

And now, what *is* the real reason why we do not seek God with all our hearts, and devote ourselves to His service, if the absence of miracles be not the reason, as most assuredly it is not? What was it that made the Israelites disobedient, who *had* miracles? St. Paul informs us, and exhorts *us* in consequence. "Harden not your hearts, *as* in the provocation, in the day of temptation in the wilderness . . . take heed . . . lest there be in any of *you*" (as there was among the Jews) "an evil heart of unbelief in departing from the Living God." Moses had been commissioned to say the same thing at the very time; "Oh that there were such a heart in them, that they would fear Me, and keep My Commandments always!" We cannot serve God, because we want the will and the heart to serve Him. We like any thing better than religion, as the Jews before us. The Jews liked this world; they liked mirth and feasting. "The people sat down to eat and to drink, and rose up to play;" so do we. They liked glitter and show, and the world's fashions. "Give us a king like the nations," they said to Samuel; so do we. They wished to be let alone; they liked ease; they liked their own way; they disliked to make war against the natural impulses and leanings of their own minds; they disliked to attend to the state of their souls, to have to treat themselves as spiritually sick and infirm, to watch, and rule, and chasten, and refrain, and change themselves; and so do we. They disliked to think of God,

and to observe and attend His ordinances, and to reverence Him; they called it a weariness to frequent His
courts; and they found this or that false worship more
pleasant, satisfactory, congenial to their feelings, than
the service of the Judge of quick and dead; and so do
we: and therefore we disobey God as they did,—not
that we have not miracles; for they actually had them,
and it made no difference. We act as they did, though
they had miracles, and we have not; because there is
one cause of it *common* both to them and us—heartlessness
in religious matters, an evil heart of unbelief; both they
and we disobey and disbelieve, because we do not love.

But this is not all; in another respect we are really
far more favoured than they were; they had outward
miracles; we too have miracles, but they are not
outward but inward. Ours are not miracles of evidence, but of power and influence. They are secret,
and more wonderful and efficacious because secret.
Their miracles were wrought upon external nature;
the sun stood still, and the sea parted. Ours are
invisible, and are exercised upon the soul. They consist in the sacraments, and they just do that very
thing which the Jewish miracles did not. They really
touch the heart, though we so often resist their influence. If then we sin, as, alas! we do, if we do
not love God more than the Jews did, if we have no
heart for those "good things which pass men's understanding," we are not more excusable than they, but

less so. For the supernatural works which God showed to them were wrought outwardly, not inwardly, and did not influence the will; they did but convey warnings; but the supernatural works which He does towards us are in the heart, and impart grace; and if we disobey, we are not disobeying His command only, but resisting His presence.

This is our state; and perhaps so it is that, as the Israelites for forty years hardened their hearts in the wilderness, in spite of the manna and the quails, and the water from the rock, so we for a course of years have been hardening ours in spite of the spiritual gifts which are the portion of Christians. Instead of listening to the voice of conscience, instead of availing ourselves of the aid of heavenly grace, we have gone on year after year with the vain dream of turning to God some future day. Childhood and boyhood are past; youth, perhaps middle age, perhaps old age is come; and now we find that we cannot "love the thing which God commandeth, and desire that which He doth promise;" and then, instead of laying the blame where it is due, on ourselves, for having hardened ourselves against the influences of grace, we complain that enough has not been done for us; we complain we have not enough light, enough help, enough inducements; we complain we have not seen miracles. Alas! how exactly are God's words fulfilled in us, which He deigned to speak to His former people. " O inhabitants of Jerusalem, and men of Judah, judge, I pray you, betwixt Me and My vineyard. What could have been done more to My vineyard that I have not done in it? wherefore, when I looked that it should bring forth grapes, brought it forth wild grapes[1]?"

Let us then put aside vain excuses; and, instead of looking for outward events to change our course of life, be sure of this, that if our course of life is to be changed, it must be from within. God's grace moves us from within, so does our own will. External circumstances have no real power over us. If we do not love God, it is because we have not wished to love Him, tried to love Him, prayed to love Him. We have not borne the idea and the wish in our mind day by day, we have not had it before us in the little matters of the day, we have not lamented that we loved Him not, we have been too indolent, sluggish, carnal, to attempt to love Him in little things, and begin at the beginning; we have shrunk from the effort of moving from within; we have been like persons who cannot get themselves to rise in the morning; and we have desired and waited for a thing impossible,—to be changed once and for all, all at once, by some great excitement from without, or some great event, or some special season; something or other we go on expecting, which is to change us without our having the trouble to change ourselves. We covet some miraculous warning, or we complain that we are

[1] Isa. v. 3, 4.

not in happier circumstances, that we have so many cares, or so few religious privileges; or we look forward for a time when religion will come easy to us as a matter of course.   This we used to look out for as boys; we used to think there was time enough yet to think of religion, and that it was a natural thing, that it came without trouble or effort, for men to be religious as life went on; we fancied that all old persons must be religious; and now even, as grown men, we have not put off this deceit; but, instead of giving our hearts to God, we are waiting, with Felix, for a convenient season.

Let us rouse ourselves, and act as reasonable men, before it is too late; let us understand, as a first truth in religion, that *love* of heaven is the only *way* to heaven. Sight will not move us; else why did Judas persist in covetousness in the very presence of Christ? why did Balaam, whose "eyes were opened," remain with a closed heart? why did Satan fall, when he was a bright Archangel?   Nor will reason subdue us; else why was the Gospel, in the beginning, "to the Greeks foolishness"?   Nor will excited feelings convert us; for there is one who "heareth the word, and anon with joy receiveth it;" yet "hath no root in himself," and "dureth" only "for a while."   Nor will self-interest prevail with us; or the rich man would have been more prudent, whose "ground brought forth plentifully," and would have recollected that "that night his soul" might be "required of him."   Let us understand that nothing but the love of God can make us believe in Him or obey Him; and let us pray Him, who has "prepared for them that love Him, such good things as pass man's understanding, to pour into our hearts such love towards Him, that we, loving Him above all things, may obtain His promises, which exceed all that we can desire."

SERMON VII.

Josiah, a Pattern for the Ignorant.

"Because thine heart was tender, and thou hast humbled thyself before the Lord, when thou heardest what I spake against this place, and against the inhabitants thereof, that they should become a desolation and a curse, and hast rent thy clothes, and wept before Me; I also have heard thee, saith the Lord. Behold therefore, I will gather thee unto thy fathers, and thou shalt be gathered into thy grave in peace; and thine eyes shall not see all the evil which I will bring upon this place."
—2 KINGS xxii. 19, 20.

KING JOSIAH, to whom these words are addressed, was one of the most pious of the Jewish kings, and the most eminent reformer of them all. On him, the last sovereign of David's house (for his sons had not an independent rule), descended the zeal and prompt obedience which raised the son of Jesse from the sheepfold to the throne, as a man after God's own heart. Thus, as an honour to David, the blessing upon his posterity remained in its fulness even to the end; its light not waxing "dim," nor "its natural force abating."

Both the character and the fortunes of Josiah are

described in the text; his character, in its saying that his "heart was tender," and that he feared God; and his fortunes, viz. an untimely death, designed as a reward for his obedience: and the text is a part of the answer which the Prophetess Huldah was instructed to make to him, when he applied for encouragement and guidance after accidentally finding the book of Moses' Law in the Temple. This discovery is the most remarkable occurrence of his reign, and will fitly serve to introduce and connect together what I wish now to set before you concerning Josiah.

The discovery of Moses' Law in the Temple is a very important occurrence in the history, because it shows us that Holy Scripture had been for a long while neglected, and to all practical purposes lost. By the book of the law is meant, I need scarcely say, the five books of Moses, which stand first in the Bible. These made up one book or volume, and were to a Jew the most important part of the Old Testament, as containing the original covenant between God and His people, and explaining to them what their place was in the scheme of God's providence, what were their duties, and what their privileges. Moses had been directed to enforce the study of this law on the Israelites in various ways. He exhorts them to "lay up his words in their heart and in their soul, and to bind them for a sign upon their hand, that they might be as frontlets between their eyes." "And ye shall teach them your children," he proceeds,

" speaking of them when thou sittest in thine house, and
when thou walkest by the way, when thou liest down,
and when thou risest up.   And thou shalt write them
upon the door-posts of thine house, and upon thy
gates [1]."   Besides this general provision, it was ordered
that once in seven years the law should be read to the
whole people assembled at the feast of tabernacles [2].
And further still, it was provided, that in case they
ever had kings, each king was to write out the whole
of it from the original copy which was kept in the ark.
" And it shall be with him, and he shall read therein all
the days of his life . . . that his heart be not lifted up
above his brethren, and that he turn not aside from the
commandment, to the right hand or to the left ; to the
end that he may prolong his days in his kingdom, he,
and his children, in the midst of Israel [3]."

However, considering how soon the nation fell into a
general disregard of the law and worship which God
gave them, it is not wonderful that these wholesome
precepts were neglected, which could not be performed
without testifying against their multiplied transgressions.   And much more when they took to themselves
idols, did they neglect, of course, to read the law which
condemned them.   And when they had set a king over
them against the will of God, it is not strange that
their kings, in turn, should neglect the direction given

Deut. xi. 18—20.   [2] Deut. xxxi. 9—13.

[3] Deut. xvii. 19, 20.

them to copy out the law for themselves; such kings especially as fell into idolatry.

All this applies particularly to the age in which Josiah succeeded to the throne, so that it is in no way surprising that he knew nothing of the law till it was by chance found in the Temple some years after his accession. The last good king of Judah before him was Hezekiah, who had been dead sixty or seventy years. That religious king had been succeeded by his son Manasseh, the most profane of all the line of David. He it was who committed those inexpiable sins which sealed the sentence of Judah's destruction. He had set up an idol in the Temple; had made his son pass through the fire; had dealt with familiar spirits and wizards; had " shed innocent blood very much, till he had filled Jerusalem from one end to another;" in a word, had " done wickedly above all that the Amorites did which were before him[1]." On his return from captivity in Babylon, whither he was taken captive, Manasseh attempted a reformation; but, alas! he found it easier to seduce than to reclaim his people[2]. Amon, who succeeded him, followed the first ways of his father during his short reign. Instead of repenting, as his father had done, he " trespassed more and more[3]." After a while, his subjects conspired and slew him. Josiah was the son of this wicked king.

Here, then, we have sufficient explanation of Josiah's

[1] 2 Kings xxi. 11.   [2] 2 Chron. xxxiii. 15—25.   [3] Ibid. 23.

ignorance of the law of Moses. He was brought up among very wicked men—in a corrupt court—after an apostasy of more than half a century; far from God's Prophets, and in the midst of idols.

In such times was Josiah born; and, like Manasseh, he came to the throne in his boyhood. As if to show us that religion depends on a man's self (under God, who gives grace), on the state of his heart, not on outward circumstances, Manasseh was the son of the pious Hezekiah, and Josiah was the son of wicked Amon. Josiah was but eight years old when his father was slain. We hear nothing of his boyhood; but scarcely was he of age to think for himself, and to profess himself a servant of the true God, but he chose that "good part which could not be taken away from him [1]." "In the eighth year of his reign" (i. e. when he was sixteen years of age), "while he was yet young, he began to seek after the God of David his father [2]." Blessed are they who so seek, for they shall find. Josiah had not the aid of a revealed volume, at least not of the Law; he was surrounded by the diversities of idol-worship, the sophistries of unbelief, the seductions of sinful pleasure. He had every temptation to go wrong; and had he done so, we might have made allowances, and said that he was not so bad as the other kings, for he knew no better; he had not sinned against light. Yes, he would have sinned against light—the event shows it; for if he

[1] Luke x. 42.   [2] 2 Chron. xxxiv. 3.

had light enough to go right (which he had, for he did go right), it follows, that if he had gone wrong, it would have been against light. Not, indeed, so strong and clear a light as Solomon disobeyed, or Joash; still against his better knowledge. This is very important. Every one, even the poorest and most ignorant, has knowledge enough to be religious. Education does not make a man religious : nor, again, is it an excuse for a man's disobedience, that he has not been educated in his duty. It only makes him less guilty than those who have been educated; that is all : he is still guilty. Here, I say, the poorest and most unlearned among us, may take a lesson from a Jewish king. Scarcely can any one in a Christian land be in more disadvantageous circumstances than Josiah—nay, scarcely in a heathen : he had idolatry around him, and at the age he began to seek God, his mind was unformed. What, then, was it that guided him ? whence his knowledge ? He had that, which all men have, heathen as well as Christians, till they pervert or blunt it—a natural sense of right and wrong; and he did not blunt it. In the words of the text, "his heart was *tender;*" he acknowledged a constraining force in the Divine voice within him—he heard and obeyed. Though all the world had told him otherwise, he could not believe and would not, that he might sin without offence —with impunity; that he might be sensual, or cruel, after the manner of idolaters, and nothing would come

of it. And further, amid all the various worships
offered to his acceptance, this same inward sense of
his, strengthened by practice, unhesitatingly chose out
the true one, the worship of the God of Israel. It
chose between the better and the worse, though it
could not have discovered the better of itself. Thus
he was led right. In his case was fulfilled the promise,
" Who is among you that feareth the Lord, that obeyeth
the voice of His servant, that walketh in darkness, and
hath no light? Let him trust in the name of the Lord,
and stay upon his God [1]." Or, in the Psalmist's words,
" The fear of the Lord is the beginning of wisdom : a
good understanding have all they that do His commandments [2]." Or (as he elsewhere expresses it), "I understand more than the ancients, because I keep Thy
precepts [3]."

Such was the beginning of Josiah's life. At sixteen
he began to seek after the God of his fathers; at
twenty he commenced his reformation, with a resolute
faith and true-hearted generous devotion. From the
language of Scripture, it would seem, he began of
himself; thus he is left a pattern to all ages of
prompt obedience for conscience' sake. Jeremiah did
not begin to prophesy till *after* the king entered on
his reformation, as if the great prophet's call were
delayed on purpose to try the strength of Josiah's
loyalty to his God, while his hands were yet unaided

[1] Isa. l. 10.   [2] Ps. cxi. 10.   [3] Ps. cxix. 100.

by the exertions of others, or by the guidance of
inspired men.

What knowledge of God's dealings with his nation
and of His revealed purposes Josiah had at this time,
we can only conjecture; from the priests he might
learn much generally, and from the popular belief.
The miraculous destruction of Sennacherib's army was
not so long since, and it proved to him God's especial
protection of the Jewish people. Manasseh's repentance
was more recent still; and the Temple itself, and its
service, contained much doctrine to a religious mind,
even apart from the law or the prophets. But he had
no accurate knowledge.

At twenty, then, he commenced his reformation. At
first, not having the Book of the Law to guide him,
he took such measures as natural conscience suggested;
he put away idolatry generally. Thus he set out, not
knowing whither he went. But it is the rule of God's
providence, that those who act up to their light, shall
be rewarded with clearer light. To him that hath,
more shall be given. Accordingly, while he was thus
engaged, after a few years, he found the Book of the Law
in the *course* of his reformations. He was seeking God
in the way of His commandments, and God met him
there. He set about repairing the Temple; and it was
in the course of this pious work that the high priest
found a copy of the Law of Moses in the Temple,

probably the original copy which was placed in the ark. Josiah's conduct on this discovery marks his character. Many men, certainly many young men, who had been so zealous as he had already shown himself for six years, would have prided themselves on what they had done, and though they began humbly, by this time would have become self-willed, self-confident, and hard-hearted. He had already been engaged in repressing and punishing God's enemies—this had a tendency to infect him with spiritual pride : and he had a work of destruction to do—this, too, might have made him cruel. Far from it : his peculiar praise is singleness of mind, a pure conscience. Even after years of activity against idolatry, in the words of the text, "his heart was tender," and he still "humbled himself before God." He felt full well the immeasurable distance between himself and his Maker; he felt his own blindness and weakness; and he still earnestly sought to know his duty better than he did, and to practise it more entirely. His was not that stern enthusiasm which has displayed itself in some so-called reformations, fancying itself God's peculiar choice, and "despising others." Here we have the pattern of reformers; singleness of heart, gentleness of temper, in the midst of zeal, resoluteness, and decision in action. All God's Saints have this union of opposite graces; Joseph, Moses, Samuel, David, Nehemiah, St. Paul : but in which of them all is the wonder-working

power of grace shown more attractively than in Josiah?
" Out of the strong came forth sweetness [1] ;" or perhaps,
as we may say more truly, Out of the sweet came forth
strength.

Observe, then, his conduct when the Law was read to
him : " When the king had heard the words of the book
of the law, *he rent his clothes* [2]." He thought far more
of what he had not done, than of what he had done.
He felt how incomplete his reformation had been; and
he felt how far more guilty his whole people were than
he had supposed, receiving, as they had, such precise
guidance in Scripture what to do, and such solemn
command to do it; and he learned, moreover, the fearful
punishment which was hanging over them ; for in that
Book of the Law were contained the threats of vengeance
to be fulfilled in case of transgression. The passages
read to him by the high priest seem to have been some
of those contained in the Book of Deuteronomy, in
which Moses sets good and evil before the people, to
choose their portion. " See, I have set before thee this
day life and good, and death and evil. . . . . I call
heaven and earth to record this day against you, that I
have set before you life and death, blessing and cursing [3]." " A blessing and a curse; a blessing if ye obey
the commandments of the Lord your God : . . . a curse
if ye will not obey [4]." And there was more than the

[1] Judges xiv. 14.

[2] 2 Kings xxii. 11.

[3] Deut. xxx. 15. 19.

[4] Deut. xi. 26—28.

mere words to terrify him; there had been a fulfilment
of them. Samaria, the ten revolting tribes, the kingdom of Israel, had been led away captive. Doubtless
he already knew that their sins had caused it; but he
found in the Book of the Law that it had been even
threatened them beforehand as the punishment; and he
discovered that the same punishment awaited his own
people, should they persist in sin. Nay, a judgment
had already taken place in Judah; for Manasseh, his
grandfather, had been carried away into Babylon, and
only restored upon his repentance.

In the twenty-eighth chapter of Deuteronomy, you
will see what was to be the curse of disobedience:
or again, consider the words of the twenty-ninth chapter: "Ye stand this day all of you before the Lord
your God . . . that thou shouldest enter into covenant with Him, and into His oath; . . . neither with
you *only* do I make this covenant and this oath; but
with him that standeth here with us this day before
the Lord our God, and *also* with him that is not here
with us this day: . . . lest there should be among
you man, or woman, or family, or tribe, whose heart
turneth away this day from the Lord our God" (alas!
as it had happened in the event, even all *ten* tribes, and
then the whole twelve had fallen away) "to go and
serve the gods of these nations; lest there should be
among you a root that beareth gall and wormwood;
and it come to pass, when he heareth the words of this

curse, that he bless himself in his heart, saying, I shall have peace, though I walk in the imagination of mine heart, to add drunkenness to thirst: the Lord will not spare him, but then the anger of the Lord and His jealousy shall smoke against that man, and all the curses that are written in this book shall lie upon him, . . . so that . . . the strangers that shall come from a far land . . . when they see the plagues of that land, and the sicknesses which the Lord hath laid upon it . . . that it is not sown, nor beareth, nor any grass groweth therein, . . . even all nations shall say, Wherefore hath the Lord done thus unto this land? what meaneth the heat of this great anger? Then men shall say, Because they have forsaken the covenant of the Lord God of their fathers, . . . for they went and served other gods, . . . and the Lord rooted them out of their land in anger, and cast them into another land." These words, or such as these, either about the people or relating to his own duties[1], Josiah read in the Book of the Law; and thinking of the captivity which had over-taken Israel already, and the sins of his own people Judah, he rent his clothes. Then he bade the priests inquire of God for him what he ought to do to avert His anger. "Go," he said, "inquire of the Lord for me, and for them that are left in Israel and in Judah, con-cerning the words of the book that is found: for great is the wrath of the Lord that is poured out upon us,

[1] Vide Deut. xvii.

because our fathers have not kept the word of the Lord,
to do after all that is written in this book[1]."

It is observable, that not even yet does he seem to
have known the prophets Jeremiah or Zephaniah, though
the former had been called to his office some years. Such
was God's pleasure. And the priests and scribes about
him, though they seconded his pious designs, were in no
sense his guides: they were unacquainted with the Law
of Moses, and with the prophets, who were interpreters
of that Law. But prophets were, through God's mercy,
in every city: and though Jeremiah might be silent or
might be away, still there were revelations from God
even in Jerusalem. To one of these prophets the priests
applied. Shallum was keeper of the king's wardrobe—
his wife Huldah was known to be gifted with the spirit
of prophecy. To her they went. She answered in the
words of which the text forms a part: "Thus saith the
Lord God of Israel, Tell ye the man that sent you to
Me, Thus saith the Lord, Behold, I will bring evil upon
this place, and upon the inhabitants thereof, even all the
words of the book which the king of Judah hath read:
because they have forsaken Me, and have burnt incense
unto other gods . . . My wrath shall be kindled
against this place, and shall not be quenched. But to
the king of Judah, which sent you to inquire of the
Lord, thus shall ye say to him, Thus saith the Lord God
of Israel, as touching the words which thou hast heard;

[1] 2 Chron. xxxiv. 21.

because thine heart was tender, and thou hast humbled thyself before the Lord, when thou heardest what I spake against this place, and against the inhabitants thereof, that they should become a desolation and a curse, and hast rent thy clothes, and wept before Me; I also have heard thee, saith the Lord. Behold therefore, I will gather thee unto thy fathers, and thou shalt be gathered into thy grave in peace: and thine eyes shall not see all the evil which I will bring upon this place. And they brought the king word again."

How King Josiah conducted himself after this message I need not describe at any length. We have heard it in the First Lesson of this Service [1]. He assembled all Judah at Jerusalem, and publicly read the words of the Book of the Law; then he made all the people renew the covenant with the God of their fathers; then he proceeded more exactly in the work of reformation in Judah and Israel, keeping closely to the directions of the Law; and after that he held his celebrated passover. Thus his greater knowledge was followed by stricter obedience: his accurate attention to the whole ritual is the very praise bestowed on his passover; "Surely there was not holden such a passover from the days of the judges [2]." Whatever he did, he did it with all his heart: "Like unto him was there no king before him, that turned to the Lord with all his

---

[1] Thirteenth Sunday after Trinity.   [2] 2 Kings xxiii. 22.

heart, and with all his soul, and with all his might, according to all the Law of Moses[1]."

Passing by the particulars of his reformation, let us come to the fulfilment of the promise made to him by Huldah, as the reward of his obedience. " Behold therefore, I will gather thee to thy fathers, and thou shalt be gathered into thy grave in peace; and thine eyes shall not see all the evil which I will bring upon this place." His reward was an early death; the event proved that it was a violent one also. The king of Egypt came up against the king of Assyria through the land of Judah; Josiah, bound perhaps by an alliance to the king of Assyria, or for some strong reason unknown, opposed him; a battle followed; Josiah disguised himself that he might not be marked out for death; but his hour was come—the promise of release was to be accomplished. " And the archers shot at king Josiah; and the king said to his servants, Have me away; for I am sore wounded. His servants, therefore . . . brought him to Jerusalem; and he died, and was buried in one of the sepulchres of his fathers[2]." Thus the best king of Judah died like Ahab, the worst king of Israel; so little may we judge of God's love or displeasure by outward appearances. "The righteous perisheth, and no man layeth it to heart: and merciful men are taken away, none considering that the righteous is taken away from the evil to come. He shall enter into peace:

[1] 2 Kings xxiii. 25. [2] 2 Chron. xxxv. 23—25.

they shall rest in their beds, each one walking in his uprightness [1]."

The sacred narrative continues : " And all Judah and Jerusalem mourned for Josiah. And Jeremiah lamented for Josiah; and all the singing men and the singing women spake of Josiah in their lamentations to this day, and made them an ordinance in Israel:" probably there was a yearly commemoration of his death; and so great was the mourning at the time, that we find it referred to in the Prophet Zechariah [2] almost as a proverb. So fell the last sovereign of the house of David. God continued His promised mercies to His people through David's line till they were too corrupt to receive them; the last king of the favoured family was forcibly and prematurely cut off, in order to make way for the display of God's vengeance in the captivity of the whole nation. He was taken out of the way; they were carried off to Babylon. " Weep ye not for the dead," says the prophet, " neither bemoan him : but weep sore for him that goeth away : for he shall return no more, nor see his native country [3]." As for Josiah, as it is elsewhere written of him, " His remembrance . . . is sweet as honey in all mouths, and as music at a banquet of wine. He behaved himself uprightly in the conversion of the people, and took away the abominations of iniquity. He directed his heart unto the Lord, and in the time of the ungodly he established

[1] Isa. lvii. 1.   [2] Zech. xii. 11.   [3] Jer. xxii. 10.

the worship of God. All, except David, and Ezekias, and Josias, were defective; for they forsook the law of the Most High, even the kings of Juda failed [1]."

In conclusion, my brethren, I would have you observe in what Josiah's chief excellence lay. This is the character given him when his name is first mentioned; "He did . . . right in the sight of the Lord, and walked in all the ways of David his father, and turned not aside to the right hand or to the left [2]." He kept the narrow middle way. Now what is this strict virtue called? it is called *faith*. It is no matter whether we call it faith or conscientiousness, they are in substance one and the same: where there is faith, there is conscientiousness—where there is conscientiousness, there is faith; they may be distinguished from each other in words, but they are not divided in fact. They belong to one, and but one, habit of mind—dutifulness; they show themselves in obedience, in the careful, anxious observance of God's will, however we learn it. Hence it is that St. Paul tells us that "the just shall live by faith" under *every* dispensation of God's mercy. And this is called *faith*, because it implies a reliance on the mere word of the unseen God overpowering the temptations of sight. Whether it be we read and accept His word in Scripture (as Christians do), or His word in our conscience, the law written on the heart (as is the case with heathens); in either case, it is by following

[1] Ecclus xlix. 1—4. [2] 2 Kings xxii. 2.

it, in spite of the seductions of the world around us, that we please God. St. Paul calls it faith; saying after the prophet, "The just shall live by faith:" and St. Peter, in the tenth chapter of the Acts, calls it "fearing and *working righteousness*," where he says, that "in every nation he that feareth God and worketh righteousness is accepted with Him." It is all one: both Apostles say that God loves those who prefer Him to the world; whose *character and frame* of mind is such. Elsewhere St. Paul also speaks like St. Peter, when he declares that God will render eternal life to them, who by "patient *continuance in* well-doing seek for glory[1]." St. John adds his testimony: "Little children, let no man deceive you. He that doeth right-eousness is righteous, even as He is righteous[2]." And our Saviour's last words at the end of the whole Scrip-ture, long after the coming of the Spirit, after the death of all the Apostles but St. John, are the same: "Blessed are they that *do His* commandments, that they may *have right* to the tree of life[3]."

And if such is God's mercy, as we trust, to all men, wherever any one with a perfect heart seeks Him, what think you is His mercy upon Christians? Something far greater, and more wonderful; for we are elected out of the world, in Jesus Christ our Saviour, to a glory incomprehensible and eternal. We are the heirs of promise; God has loved us before we were born. He

---

[1] Rom. ii. 7.   [2] 1 John iii. 7.   [3] Rev. xxii. 14.

had us taken into His Church in our infancy. He by Baptism made us new creatures, giving us powers which we by nature had not, and raising us to the unseen society of Saints and Angels. And all this we enjoy on our faith; that is, on our believing that we have them, and seriously trying to profit by them. May God grant, that we, like Josiah, may improve our gifts, and trade and make merchandise with them. so that, when He cometh to reckon with us, we may be accepted!

SERMON VIII.

Inward Witness to the Truth of the Gospel.

"I have more understanding than my teachers, for Thy testimonies are my study; I am wiser than the aged, because I keep Thy commandments."—PSALM cxix. 99, 100.

IN these words the Psalmist declares, that in consequence of having obeyed God's commandments he had obtained more wisdom and understanding than those who had first enlightened his ignorance, and were once more enlightened than he. As if he said, "When I was a child, I was instructed in religious knowledge by kind and pious friends, who told me who my Maker was, what great things He had done for me, how much I owed to Him, and how I was to serve Him. All this I learned from them, and I rejoice that they taught it me: yet they did more; they set me in the way to gain a knowledge of religious truth in another and higher manner. They not only taught me, but trained me; they were careful that I should not only know my duty, but do it. They obliged me to obey; they obliged me to begin a religious course of life, which (praised be God!) I have ever pursued; and this obedience to His commandments has brought me to a clearer knowledge of His truth, than any mere instruction could convey. I have been taught, not from without merely, but from within. I have been taught by means of a purified heart, by a changed will, by chastened reins, by a mortified appetite, by a bridled tongue, by eyes corrected and subdued. 'I have more understanding than my teachers, for Thy testimonies,' O Lord, 'are my study; I am wiser than the aged, because I keep Thy commandments.'"

We may sometimes hear men say, "How do you know that the Bible is true? You are told so in Church; your parents believed it; but might they not be mistaken? and if so, you are mistaken also." Now to this objection it may be answered, and very satisfactorily, "Is it then nothing toward convincing us of the truth of the Gospel, that those whom we love best and reverence most believe it? Is it against reason to think that they are right, who have considered the matter most deeply? Do we not receive what they tell us in other matters, though we cannot prove the truth of their information; for instance, in matters of art and science; why then is it irrational to believe them in religion also? Have not the wisest and holiest of men been Christians? and have not unbelievers, on the contrary, been very generally signal instances of pride, discontent, and

profligacy? Again, are not the principles of unbelief
certain to dissolve human society? and is not this plain
fact, candidly considered, enough to show that unbelief
cannot be a right condition of our nature? for who can
believe that we were intended to live in anarchy? If
we have no good reason for believing, at least we have
no good reason for disbelieving. If you ask why we
are Christians, we ask in turn, Why should we not be
Christians? it will be enough to remain where we are,
till you do what you never can do—prove to us for
certain, that the Gospel is not Divine; it is enough for
us to be on the side of good men, to be under the feet
of the Saints, to 'go our way forth by the footsteps of
the flock, and to feed our kids beside the shepherds'
tents[1].'"

This would be quite a sufficient answer, had we
nothing else to say; but I will give another, and that
in connexion with the text; I will show you that the
most unlearned Christian may have a very real and
substantial argument, an intimate token, of the truth of
the Gospel, quite independent of the authority of his
parents and teachers; nay, that were all the world, even
were his teachers, to tell him that religion was a dream,
still he would have a good reason for believing it true.

This reason, I say, is contained in the text—" I have
more understanding than the aged, *because* I keep Thy
commandments." By obeying the commands of Scrip-

[1] Cant. i. 8.

ture, we learn that these commands really come from God; by trying we make proof; by doing we come to know. Now how comes this to pass? It happens in several ways.

1. Consider the Bible tells us to be meek, humble, single-hearted, and teachable. Now, it is plain that humility and teachableness are qualities of mind necessary for arriving at the truth in any subject, and in religious matters as well as others. By obeying Scripture, then, in practising humility and teachableness, it is evident we are at least *in the way* to arrive at the knowledge of God. On the other hand, impatient, proud, self-confident, obstinate men, are generally wrong in the opinions they form of persons and things. Prejudice and self-conceit blind the eyes and mislead the judgment, whatever be the subject inquired into. For instance, how often do men mistake the characters and misconstrue the actions of others! how often are they deceived in them! how often do the young form acquaintances injurious to their comfort and good! how often do men embark in foolish and ruinous schemes! how often do they squander their money, and destroy their worldly prospects! And what, I ask, is so frequent a cause of these many errors as wilfulness and presumption? The same thing happens also in religious inquiries. When I see a person hasty and violent, harsh and high-minded, careless of what others feel, and disdainful of what they think;—when I see such a one

proceeding to inquire into religious subjects, I am sure beforehand he cannot go right—he will not be led into all the truth—it is contrary to the nature of things and the experience of the world, that he should find what he is seeking. I should say the same were he seeking to find out what to believe or do in any other matter not religious,—but especially in any such important and solemn inquiry; for the *fear* of the Lord (humbleness, teachableness, reverence towards Him) is the very *beginning* of wisdom, as Solomon tells us; it leads us to think over things modestly and honestly, to examine patiently, to bear doubt and uncertainty, to wait perseveringly for an increase of light, to be slow to speak, and to be deliberate in deciding.

2. Consider, in the next place, that those who are trained carefully according to the precepts of Scripture, gain an elevation, a delicacy, refinement, and sanctity of mind, which is most necessary for judging fairly of the truth of Scripture.

A man who loves sin does not wish the Gospel to be true, and therefore is not a fair judge of it; a mere man of the world, a selfish and covetous man, or a drunkard, or an extortioner, is, from a sense of interest, against that Bible which condemns him, and would account that man indeed a messenger of good tidings of peace who could prove to him that Christ's doctrine was not from God. " Every one that doeth evil hateth the light, neither cometh to the light, lest his deeds should be reproved[1]." I do not mean to say that such men necessarily reject the word of God, as if we could dare to conclude that all who do not reject it are therefore sure to be not covetous, drunkards, extortioners, and the like; for it is often a man's interest not openly to reject it, though it be against him; and the bulk of men are inconsistent, and have some good feelings left, even amid their sins and vices, which keep them from going all lengths. But, while they still profess to honour, at least they try to pervert and misinterpret Scripture, and that comes to the same thing. They try to persuade themselves that Christ will save them, though they continue in sin; or they wish to believe that future punishment will not last for ever; or they conceive that their good deeds or habits, few and miserable as they are at best, will make up for the sins of which they are too conscious. Whereas such men as have been taught betimes to work with God their Saviour—in ruling their hearts, and curbing their sinful passions, and changing their wills—though they are still sinners, have not within them that treacherous enemy of the truth which misleads the judgments of irreligious men.

Here, then, are two very good reasons at first sight, why men who obey the Scripture precepts are more likely to arrive at religious truth, than those who neglect them; first, because such men are teachable men; secondly, because they are pure in heart; such

[1] John iii. 20.

shall see God, whereas the proud provoke His anger, and the carnal are His abhorrence.

But to proceed. Consider, moreover, that those who try to obey God evidently gain a knowledge of themselves at least; and this may be shown to be the first and principal step towards knowing God. For let us suppose a child, under God's blessing, profiting by his teacher's guidance, and trying to do his duty and please God. He will perceive that there is much in him which ought not to be in him. His own natural sense of right and wrong tells him that peevishness, sullenness, deceit, and self-will, are tempers and principles of which he has cause to be ashamed, and he feels that these bad tempers and principles are in his heart. As he grows older, he will understand this more and more. Wishing, then, and striving to act up to the law of conscience, he will yet find that, with his utmost efforts, and after his most earnest prayers, he still falls short of what he knows to be right, and what he aims at. Conscience, however, being respected, will become a more powerful and enlightened guide than before; it will become more refined and hard to please; and he will understand and perceive more clearly the distance that exists between his own conduct and thoughts, and perfection. He will admire and take pleasure in the holy law of God, of which he reads in Scripture; but he will be humbled withal, as understanding himself to be a continual transgressor against it. Thus he will learn from experience the doctrine of original sin, before he knows the actual name of it. He will, in fact, say to himself, what St. Paul describes all beginners in religion as saying, " What I would, that do I not; but what I hate, that do I. I delight in the law of God after the inward man, but I see another law in my members, warring against the law of my mind, and bringing me into captivity. I know that in my flesh dwelleth no good thing [1]." The effect of this experience will be to make him take it for granted, as an elementary truth, that he cannot gain heaven for himself; to make him feel himself guilty before God; and to feel, moreover, that even were he admitted into the Divine presence, yet, till his heart be (so to say) made over again, he cannot perfectly enjoy God. This, surely, is the state of self-knowledge; these are the convictions to which every one is brought on, who attempts honestly to obey the precepts of God. I do not mean that all that I have been saying will necessarily pass through his mind, and in the same order, or that he will be conscious of it, or be able to speak of it, but that on the whole thus he will feel.

When, then, even an unlearned person thus trained— from his own heart, from the action of his mind upon itself, from struggles with self, from an attempt to follow those impulses of his own nature which he feels to be highest and noblest, from a vivid natural per-

[1] Rom. vii. 15. 18. 22, 23.

ception (natural, though cherished and strengthened by
prayer; natural, though unfolded and diversified by
practice; natural, though of that new and second nature
which God the Holy Ghost gives), from an innate,
though supernatural perception of the great vision of
Truth which is external to him (a perception of it, not
indeed in its fulness, but in glimpses, and by fits and
seasons, and in its persuasive influences, and through a
courageous following on after it, as a man in the dark
might follow after some dim and distant light)—I say,
when a person thus trained from his own heart, reads
the declarations and promises of the Gospel, are we to
be told that he believes in them merely because he has
been bid believe in them? Do we not see he has
besides this a something in his own breast which bears
a confirming testimony to their truth? He reads that
the heart is " deceitful above all things and desperately
wicked [1]," and that he inherits an evil nature from
Adam, and that he is still under its power, except so far
as he has been renewed. Here is a mystery; but his
own actual and too bitter experience bears witness to
the truth of the declaration; he feels the mystery of
iniquity within him. He reads, that " without holiness
no man shall see the Lord [2];" and his own love of what
is true and lovely and pure, approves and embraces the
doctrine as coming from God. He reads, that God is
angry at sin, and will punish the sinner, and that it is

---

[1] Jer. xvii. 9.   [2] Heb. xii. 14.

a hard matter, nay, an impossibility, for us to appease His wrath. Here, again, is a mystery : but here, too, his conscience anticipates the mystery, and convicts him; his mouth is stopped. And when he goes on to read that the Son of God has Himself come into the world in our flesh, and died upon the Cross for us, does he not, amid the awful mysteriousness of the doctrine, find those words fulfilled in him which that gracious Saviour uttered, " And I, if I be lifted up from the earth, will draw all men unto Me"? He cannot choose but believe in Him. He says, " O Lord, Thou art stronger than I, and hast prevailed."

Here then, I say, he surely possesses an evidence perfectly distinct from the authority of superiors and teachers ; like St. Paul, he is in one way not taught of men, "but by the revelation of Jesus Christ[1]." Others have but bid him look within, and pray for God's grace to be enabled to know himself; and the more he understands his own heart, the more are the Gospel doctrines recommended to his reason. He is assured that Christ does not speak of Himself, but that His word is from God. He is ready, with the Samaritan woman, to say to all around him, " Come, see a man, which told me all things that ever I did: is not this the Christ[2]?" Or, again, in the words which the Samaritans of the same city used to the woman after conversing with Christ; "Now we believe, *not* because of thy saying" (not

---

[1] Gal. i. 12.   [2] John iv. 29.

merely on the authority of friends and relatives); "for *we* have heard Him ourselves, and know that this is indeed the Christ, the Saviour of the world."

The Bible, then, seems to say,—God is not a hard master to require belief, without affording grounds for believing; only follow your own sense of right, and you will gain from that very obedience to your Maker, which natural conscience enjoins, a conviction of the truth and power of that Redeemer whom a supernatural message has revealed; do but examine your thoughts and doings; do but attempt what you know to be God's will, and you will most assuredly be led on into all the truth: you will recognize the force, meaning, and awful graciousness of the Gospel Creed; you will bear witness to the truth of one doctrine, by your own past experience of yourselves; of another, by seeing that it is suited to your necessity; of a third, by finding it fulfilled upon your obeying it. As the prophet says, "Bring ye" your offering "into Mine house," saith the Lord, "and prove Me now herewith, if I will not open you the windows of heaven, and pour you out a blessing that there shall not be room enough to receive it [1]."

My brethren, it is always reasonable to insist upon these subjects; but it is peculiarly so in times when a spirit of presumptuous doubting is in many places abroad. As many of us as live in the world must

[1] Mal. iii. 10.

expect to hear our faith despised, and our conscientious obedience ridiculed; we must expect to be taunted and scorned by those who find it much easier to attack another's creed than to state their own. A little learning is a dangerous thing. When men think they know more than others, they often talk for the sake of talking, or to show their ability (as they think), their shrewdness and depth; and they speak lightly of the All-Holy God, to gratify their empty self-conceit and vanity. And often it answers no purpose to dispute with such persons; for not having been trained up to obey their conscience, to restrain their passions, and examine their hearts, they will assent to nothing you can say; they will be questioning and arguing about every thing; they have no common ground with you, and when they talk of religion they are like blind persons talking of colours. If you urge how great a gift it is to be at peace with God, or of the arduousness and yet desirableness of perfection, or the beauty of saintliness, or the dangerousness of the world, or the blessedness of self-control, or the glory of virginity, or the answers which God gives to prayer, or the marvellousness and almost miraculousness of His providences, or the comfort of religion in affliction, or the strength given you over your passions in the Most Holy Sacrament, such persons understand you not at all. They will laugh, they will scoff, at best they will wonder: any how what you say is no evidence to *them*. You cannot convince them, because you differ from them in first principles; it is not that they start from the same point as you, and afterwards strike off in some wayward direction; but their course is altogether distinct, they have no point in common with you. For such persons then you can only pray; God alone can bring down pride, self-conceit, an arrogant spirit, a presumptuous temper; God alone can dissipate prejudice; God alone can overcome flesh and blood. Useful as argument may be for converting a man, in such cases God seldom condescends to employ it. Yet, let not such vain or ignorant reasoners convert you to unbelief in great matters or little; let them not persuade you, that your faith is built on the mere teaching of fallible men; do not you be ridiculed out of your confidence and hope in Christ. You may, if you will, have an inward witness arising from obedience: and though you cannot make them see it, you can see it yourselves, which is the great thing; and it will be quite sufficient, with God's blessing, to keep you stedfast in the way of life.

Lastly, let me remark how dangerous their state is who are content to take the truths of the Gospel on trust, without caring whether or not those truths are realized in their own heart and conduct. Such men, when assailed by ridicule and sophistry, are likely to fall; they have no root in themselves; and let them be quite sure, that should they fall away from the faith, it will be a slight thing at the last day to plead that subtle arguments were used against them, that they were altogether unprepared and ignorant, and that their seducers prevailed over them by the display of some little cleverness and human knowledge. The inward witness to the truth lodged in our hearts is a match for the most learned infidel or sceptic that ever lived : though, to tell the truth, such men are generally very shallow and weak, as well as wicked; generally know only a little, pervert what they know, assume false principles, and distort or suppress facts : but were they as accomplished as the very author of evil, the humblest Christian, armed with sling and stone, and supported by God's unseen might, is, as far as his own faith is concerned, a match for them. And, on the other hand, the most acute of reasoners and most profound of thinkers, the most instructed in earthly knowledge, is nothing, except he has also within him the presence of the Spirit of truth. Human knowledge, though of great power when joined to a pure and humble faith, is of no power when opposed to it, and, after all, for the comfort of the individual Christian, it is of little value.

May we, then, all grow in heavenly knowledge, and, with that end, labour to improve what is already given us, be it more or be it less, knowing that " he that is faithful in little is faithful also in much," and that " to him that hath, more shall be given."

SERMON IX.

Jeremiah, a Lesson for the Disappointed.

"Be not afraid of their faces: for I am with thee to deliver thee, saith the Lord."—JEREMIAH i. 8.

THE Prophets were ever ungratefully treated by the Israelites; they were resisted, their warnings neglected, their good services forgotten. But there was this difference between the earlier and the later Prophets; the earlier lived and died in honour among their people,—in outward honour; though hated and thwarted by the wicked, they were exalted to high places, and ruled in the congregation. Moses, for instance, was in trouble from his people all his life long, but to the end he was their lawgiver and judge. Samuel, too, even though rejected, was still held in reverence; and when he died, "all the Israelites were gathered together and lamented him, and buried him in his house at Ramah [1]." David died on a royal throne. But in the latter times, the prophets were

[1] 1 Sam. xxv. 1.

not only feared and hated by the enemies of God, but cast out of the vineyard. As the time approached for the coming of the true Prophet of the Church, the Son of God, they resembled Him in their earthly fortunes more and more; and as He was to suffer, so did they. Moses was a ruler, Jeremiah was an outcast: Samuel was buried in peace, John the Baptist was beheaded. In St. Paul's words, they " had trial of cruel mockings and scourgings, yea, moreover, of bonds and imprisonment. They were stoned; they were sawn asunder, were tempted, were slain with the sword; they wandered about in sheepskins and goatskins, being destitute, afflicted, tormented; of whom the world was not worthy; they wandered in deserts, and in mountains, and in dens and caves of the earth [1]."

Of these, Elijah, who lived in the wilderness, and the hundred prophets whom Obadiah fed by fifty in a cave, are examples of the wanderers. And Micaiah, who was appointed the bread of affliction and the water of affliction by an idolatrous king, is the specimen of those who " had trial of bonds and imprisonment." Of those who were sawn asunder and slain with the sword, Isaiah is the chief, who, as tradition goes, was by order of Manasseh, the son of Hezekiah, sawn asunder with a wooden saw. And of those who were stoned, none is more famous than Zechariah, the son of Jehoiada, " who was slain between the temple and the altar [2]." But of

[1] Heb. xi. 36—38.　　　　[2] Matt. xxiii. 35.

all the persecuted prophets Jeremiah is the most eminent; i. e. we know more of his history, of his imprisonments, his wanderings, and his afflictions. He may be taken as a representative of the Prophets; and hence it is that he is an especial type of our Lord and Saviour. All the Prophets were types of the Great Prophet whose way they were preparing; they tended towards and spoke of Christ. In their sufferings they foreshadowed His priesthood, and in their teaching His prophetical office, and in their miracles His royal power. The history of Jeremiah, then, as being drawn out in Scripture more circumstantially than that of the other Prophets, is the most exact type of Christ among them; that is, next to David, who, of course, was the nearest resemblance to Him of all, as a sufferer, an inspired teacher, and a king. Jeremiah comes next to David; I do not say in dignity and privilege, for it was Elijah who was taken up to heaven, and appeared at the Transfiguration; nor in inspiration, for to Isaiah one should assign the higher evangelical gifts; but in typifying Him who came and wept over Jerusalem, and then was tortured and put to death by those He wept over. And hence, when our Lord came, while some thought Him Elijah, and others John the Baptist, risen from the dead, there were others who thought Him Jeremiah. Of Jeremiah, then, I will now speak, as a specimen of all those Prophets whom St. Paul sets before us as examples of faith, and St. James as examples of patience.

Jeremiah's ministry may be summed up in three words, good hope, labour, disappointment.

It was his privilege to be called to his sacred office from his earliest years. Like Samuel, the first prophet, he was of the tribe of Levi, dedicated from his birth to religious services, and favoured with the constant presence and grace of God. "Before I formed thee . . . . I knew thee[1]," says the word of the Lord to him when He gave him his commission, "and before thou camest out of the womb I sanctified thee, and I ordained thee a prophet unto the nations." This commission was given the year after Josiah began his reformation. Jeremiah returned for answer, "Ah! Lord God! behold, I cannot speak; for I am a child." He felt the arduousness of a prophet's office; the firmness and intrepidity which were required to speak the words of God. "But the Lord said unto him, Say not I am a child; for thou shalt go to all that I shall send thee, and whatsoever I command thee thou shalt speak. Be not afraid of their faces, for I am with thee to deliver thee, saith the Lord. Then the Lord put forth His hand and touched my mouth, and said unto me, Behold I have put My words in thy mouth."

No prophet commenced his labours with greater encouragement than Jeremiah. A king had succeeded to the throne who was bringing back the times of the man after God's own heart. There had not been a son

[1] Jer. i. 5.

of David so zealous as Josiah since David himself. The king, too, was young, at most twenty years of age, in the beginning of his reformation. What might not be effected in a course of years, however corrupt and degraded was the existing state of his people? So Jeremiah might think. It must be recollected, too, that religious obedience was under the Jewish covenant awarded with temporal prosperity. There seemed, then, every reason for Jeremiah at first to suppose that bright fortunes were in store for the Church. Josiah was the very king whose birth was foretold by name above three hundred years before, when Jeroboam established idolatry; who was the promised avenger of God's covenant, "the repairer of the breach, the restorer of paths to dwell in [1]." Israel (the ten tribes) having gone into captivity, schism had come to its end; the kings of the house of David again ruled over the whole extent of the promised land; idolatry was destroyed by Josiah in all the cities. Such were the present blessings which the Jewish remnant enjoyed. At first sight, then, it seemed reasonable to anticipate further and permanent improvement. Every one begins with being sanguine; doubtless then, as now, many labourers in God's husbandry entered on their office with more lively hopes than their after fortunes warranted. Whether or not, however, such hope of success encouraged Jeremiah's first exertions, very soon, in his case, this cheerful prospect was

[1] Isa. lviii. 12.

overcast, and he was left to labour in the dark. Huldah's message to the king, on his finding the Book of the Law in the temple, fixed the coming fortunes of Judah. Huldah foretold a woe,—an early removal of the good Josiah to his rest as a mercy to him, and to the nation, who were unworthy of him, a fierce destruction. This prophecy was delivered five years after Jeremiah entered upon his office; he ministered in all forty years before the captivity; so early in his course were his hopes cut away.

But even though Huldah's message be supposed not to reach him, still he was doubtless soon undeceived as to any hopes he might entertain, whether, by the express Word of God informing him, or by the actual hardened state of sin in which the nation lay. Soon, surely, were his hopes destroyed, and his mind sobered into a more blessed and noble temper,—resignation.

I call resignation a more blessed frame of mind than sanguine hope of present success, because it is the truer, and the more consistent with our fallen state of being, and the more improving to our hearts; and because it is that for which the most eminent servants of God have been conspicuous. To expect great effects from our exertions for religious objects is natural indeed, and innocent, but it arises from inexperience of the kind of work we have to do,—to change the heart and will of man. It is a far nobler frame of mind, to labour, not with the hope of seeing the fruit of our labour, but for

[VIII]   K

conscience' sake, as a matter of duty; and again, in
faith, trusting good *will* be done, though we see it not.
Look through the Bible, and you will find God's servants, even though they began with success, end with
disappointment; not that God's purposes or His instru-
ments fail, but that the time for reaping what we have
sown is hereafter, not here; that here there is no great
visible fruit in any one man's lifetime. Moses, for instance, began with leading the Israelites out of Egypt in
triumph; he ended at the age of an hundred and twenty
years, before his journey was finished and Canaan gained,
one among the offending multitudes who were over-
thrown in the wilderness [1]. Samuel's reformations ended
in the people's wilfully choosing a king like the nations
around them. Elijah, after his successes, fled from Jezebel
into the wilderness to mourn over his disappointments.
Isaiah, after Hezekiah's religious reign, and the miraculous destruction of Sennacherib's army, fell upon the
evil days of his son Manasseh. Even in the successes of
the first Christian teachers, the Apostles, the same rule
is observed. After all the great works God enabled
them to accomplish, they confessed before their death
that what they experienced, and what they saw before
them, was reverse and calamity, and that the fruit of
their labour would not be seen, till Christ came to open
the books and collect His saints from the four corners of
the earth. "Evil men and seducers shall wax worse

[1] 1 Cor. x. 5.

and worse, deceiving and being deceived[1]," is the testimony of St. Peter, St. Paul, St. John, and St. Jude.

Now, in the instance of Jeremiah, we have on record that variety and vicissitude of feelings, which this transition from hope to disappointment produces, at least in a sensitive mind. His trials were very great, even in Josiah's reign; but when that pious king's countenance was withdrawn on his early death, he was exposed to persecution from every class of men. At one time we read of the people conspiring against him[2]; at another, of the men of his own city, Anathoth, "seeking his life[3]," on account of his prophesying in the Lord's name. At another time he was seized by the priests and the prophets in order to be put to death, from which he was only saved by certain of the princes and elders who were still faithful to the memory of Josiah[4]. Then, again, Pashur, the chief governor of the temple, smote him and tortured him[5]. At another time, the king, Zedekiah, put him in prison[6]. Afterwards, when the army of the Chaldeans had besieged Jerusalem, the Jews accused him of falling away to the enemy[7], and smote him, and imprisoned him; then they cast him into a dungeon, where he "sunk in the mire," and almost perished from hunger[8]. When Jerusalem had been taken by the enemy, Jeremiah was forcibly carried

[1] 2 Tim. iii. 13.   [2] Jer. xviii. 18.   [3] Ibid. xi. 21.
[4] Ibid. xxvi. 16, &c.   [5] Ibid. xx. 2.   [6] Ibid. xxxii. 3.
[7] Ibid. xxxvii. 14.   [8] Ibid. xxxviii. 6. 9.

down to Egypt by men who at first pretended to reverence and consult him [1], and there he came to his end—it is believed, a violent end. Nebuchadnezzar, the heathen king of Babylon and conqueror of Jerusalem, was one of the few persons who showed him kindness. This great king, who afterwards honoured Daniel, and was at length brought to acknowledge the God of heaven by a severe chastisement, on the taking of the city delivered Jeremiah from prison [2], and gave charge to the captain of his guard concerning him, to "look well to him, and to do him no harm; but to do unto him even as he should say . . . ." An Ethiopian, another heathen, is also mentioned as delivering him from the dungeon.

Such were his trials: his affliction, fear, despondency, and sometimes even restlessness under them are variously expressed; that succession and tide of feelings which most persons undergo before their minds settle into the calm of resignation. At one time he speaks as astonished at his failure: "O Lord, art not Thine eyes upon the truth? Thou hast stricken them, but they have not grieved; Thou hast consumed them, but they have refused to receive correction [3]." Again, "A wonderful and horrible thing is committed in the land; the prophets prophesy falsely, and the priests bear rule by their means; and My people love to have it so [4]." At another time, he expresses his perplexity at the

---

[1] Jer. xlii. xliii.   [2] Ibid. xxxix. 14.
[3] Ibid. v. 3.   [4] Ibid. v. 30, 31.

disorder of the world, and the successes of the wicked: " Righteous art Thou, O Lord, when I plead with Thee; yet let me talk with Thee of Thy judgments: wherefore doth the way of the wicked prosper? wherefore are all they happy that deal very treacherously? . . . . but Thou, O Lord, knowest me; Thou hast seen me, and tried mine heart towards Thee[1]." Then, in turn, his mind frets at the thought of its own anxious labours and perplexities: " Woe is me, my mother, that thou hast borne me a man of strife and a man of contention to the whole earth! I have neither lent on usury, nor men have lent to me on usury; yet every one of them doth curse me. . . . . Why is my pain perpetual, and my wound incurable? . . . wilt Thou be altogether unto me as a deceiver, and as waters that fail[2]?" These are the sorrows of a gentle and peaceable mind, forced against its will into the troubles of life, and incurring the hatred of those whom it opposes against its nature. This he elsewhere expresses thus: " As for me, I have not . . . desired the woeful day" (which he foretold); " Thou knowest: that which came out of my lips was right before Thee. Be not a terror unto me: Thou art my hope in the day of evil[3]." When Pashur put him to torture he was still more agitated, and said, " O Lord, Thou hast deceived me, and I was deceived. Thou art stronger than I, and hast prevailed. I am in derision daily, every one mocketh me. . . . Cursed be the day

[1] Jer. xii. 1—3.   [2] Ibid. xv. 10—18.   [3] Ibid. xvii. 16, 17.

wherein I was born" (here certainly is the language even of impatience), "let not the day wherein my mother bare me be blessed[1]."

However, of such changes of feelings what was the end?—resignation. He elsewhere uses language which expresses that chastened spirit and weaned heart, which is the termination of all agitation and anxiety in the case of religious minds. He, who at one time could not comfort himself, at another was sent to comfort a brother; and, in comforting Baruch, he speaks in that nobler temper of resignation which takes the place of sanguine hope and harassing fear, and betokens calm and clear-sighted faith and inward peace. "Thus saith the Lord the God of Israel unto thee, O Baruch. Thou didst say, Woe is me now, for the Lord hath added grief to my sorrow; I fainted in my sighing, and I find no rest. . . . . Behold, that which I have built will I break down, and that which I have planted I will pluck up, even this whole land. And seekest thou great things for thyself? seek them not: for, behold, I will bring evil upon all flesh; . . . but thy life will I give unto thee for a prey in all places whither thou goest;" that is, seek not success, be not impatient, fret not thyself—be content, if, after all thy labours, thou dost but save thyself, without seeing other fruit of them.

And now, my brethren, does what I have been saying

[1] Jer. xx. 7—14.

apply to all of us, or only to Prophets? It applies to all of us. For all of us live in a world which promises well, but does not fulfil; and all of us (taking our lives altogether apart from religious prospects) begin with hope, and end with disappointment. Doubtless, there is much difference in our respective trials here, arising from difference of tempers and fortunes. Still it is in our nature to begin life thoughtlessly and joyously; to seek great things in one way or other; to have vague notions of good to come; to love the world, and to believe its promises, and seek satisfaction and happiness from it. And, as it is our nature to hope, so it is our lot, as life proceeds, to encounter disappointment. I know that there are multitudes, in the retired ranks of society, who pass their days without any great varieties of fortune; though, even in such cases, thinking persons will have much more to say of themselves than at first sight might appear. Still, that disappointment in some shape or other is the lot of man (that is, looking at our prospects apart from the next world) is plain, from the mere fact, if nothing else could be said, that we begin life with health and end it with sickness; or in other words, that it *comes* to an *end*, for an end is a failure. And even in the quietest walks of life, do not the old feel regret, more or less vividly, that they are not young? Do not they lament the days gone by, and even with the pleasure of remembrance feel the pain? And why, except that they think that they have lost something which they once had, whereas in the beginning of life, they thought of gaining something they had not? A double disappointment.

Now is it religion that suggests this sad view of things? No, it is experience; it is the *world's* doing; it is fact, from which we cannot escape, though the Bible said not a word about the perishing nature of all earthly pleasures.

Here then it is, that God Himself offers us His aid by His Word, and in His Church. Left to ourselves, we seek good from the world, but cannot find it; in youth we look forward, and in age we look back. It is well we should be persuaded of these things betimes, to gain wisdom and to provide for the evil day. Seek we great things? We must seek them where they really are to be found, and in the way in which they are to be found; we must seek them as He has set them before us, who came into the world to enable us to gain them. We must be willing to give up present hope for future enjoyment, this world for the unseen. The truth is (though it is so difficult for us to admit it heartily), our nature is not at first in a state to enjoy happiness, even if we had it offered to us. We seek for it, and we feel we need it; but (strange though it is to say, still so it is) we are not fitted to be happy. If then at once we rush forward to seek enjoyment, it will be like a child's attempting to walk before his strength is come. If we would gain true bliss, we must cease to seek it as an end; we must postpone the prospect of enjoying it. For we are by nature in an unnatural state; we must be changed from what we are when born, before we can receive our greatest good. And as in sickness sharp remedies are often used, or irksome treatment, so it is with our souls; we must go through pain, we must practise self-denial, we must curb our wills, and purify our hearts, before we are capable of any lasting solid peace. To attempt to gain happiness, except in this apparently tedious and circuitous way, is a labour lost; it is building on the sand; the foundation will soon give way, though the house looks fair for a time. To be gay and thoughtless, to be self-indulgent and self-willed, is quite out of character with our real state. We must learn to know ourselves, and to have thoughts and feelings becoming ourselves. Impetuous hope and un-disciplined mirth ill-suit a sinner. Should *he* shrink from low notions of himself, and sharp pain, and mortifi-cation of natural wishes, whose guilt called down the Son of God from heaven to die upon the cross for him? May he live in pleasure here, and call this world his home, while he reads in the Gospel of his Saviour's life-long affliction and disappointment?

It cannot be; let us prepare for suffering and dis-appointment, which befit us as sinners, and which are necessary for us as saints. Let us not turn away from trial when God brings it on us, or play the coward in the fight of faith. " Watch ye, stand fast in the faith,

quit you like men, be strong[1];" such is St. Paul's
exhortation. When affliction overtakes you, remember
to accept it as a means of improving your hearts, and
pray God for His grace that it may do so. Look disappointment in the face. "Take . . . . the Prophets
. . . . for an example of suffering affliction, and of
patience. Behold, we count them happy who endure."
Give not over your attempts to serve God, though you
see nothing come of them. Watch and pray, and obey
your conscience, though you cannot perceive your own
progress in holiness. Go on, and you cannot but go
forward; believe it, though you do not see it. Do the
duties of your calling, though they are distasteful to
you. Educate your children carefully in the good way,
though you cannot tell how far God's grace has touched
their hearts. Let your light shine before men, and
praise God by a consistent life, even though others do
not seem to glorify their Father on account of it, or to
be benefited by your example. "Cast your bread upon
the waters, for you shall find it after many days. . . . .
In the morning sow your seed, in the evening withhold
not your hand; for you know not whether shall prosper,
either this or that; or whether they both shall be alike
good[2]." Persevere in the narrow way. The Prophets
went through sufferings to which ours are mere trifles;
violence and craft combined to turn them aside, but
they kept right on, and are at rest.

[1] 1 Cor. xvi. 13.   [2] Eccl. xi. 1. 6.

Now, I know full well, that this whole subject is distasteful to many men, who say we ought to be cheerful. "We are bid rejoice, why then do you bid us mourn?" I bid you mourn in order that you may rejoice more perfectly. "Blessed are they that mourn, for they shall be comforted[1]." "They that sow in tears, shall reap in joy." I bid you take up the cross of Christ, that you may wear His crown. Give your hearts to Him, and you will for yourselves solve the difficulty, how Christians can be sorrowful, yet alway rejoicing[2]. You will find that lightness of heart and cheerfulness are quite consistent with that new and heavenly character which He gives us, though to gain it in any good measure, we must for a time be sorrowful, and ever after thoughtful. But I give you fair warning, you must at first take His word on trust; and if you do not, there is no help for it. He says, "Come unto Me, . . . and I will give you rest." You must begin on faith: you cannot see at first whither He is leading you, and how light will rise out of the darkness. You must begin by denying yourselves your natural wishes,—a painful work; by refraining from sin, by rousing from sloth, by preserving your tongue from insincere words, and your hands from deceitful dealings, and your eyes from beholding vanity; by watching against the first rising of anger, pride, impurity, obstinacy, jealousy; by learning to endure the laugh of

[1] Matt. v. 4.   [2] 2 Cor. vi. 10.

irreligious men for Christ's sake; by forcing your minds to follow seriously the words of prayer, though it be difficult to you, and by keeping before you the thought of God all through the day. These things you will be able to do if you do but seek the mighty help of God the Holy Spirit which is given you; and while you follow after them, then, in the Prophet's language, "your light shall rise in obscurity, and your darkness shall be as the noonday. And the Lord shall guide you continually, and satisfy your soul in drought: and you shall be like a watered garden, and like a spring of water, whose waters fail not[1]."

[1] Isa. lviii. 10, 11.

SERMON X.

Endurance of the World's Censure.

"And thou, son of man, be not afraid of them; neither be afraid of their words, though briars and thorns be with thee, and thou dost dwell among scorpions; be not afraid of their words, nor be dismayed at their looks, though they be a rebellious house."—EZEKIEL ii. 6.

WHAT is here implied, as the trial of the Prophet Ezekiel, was fulfilled more or less in the case of all the Prophets. They were not Teachers merely, but Confessors. They came not merely to unfold the Law, or to foretell the Gospel, but to warn and rebuke; nor to rebuke only, but to suffer. This world is a scene of conflict between good and evil. The evil not only avoids, but persecutes the good; the good cannot conquer, except by suffering. Good men seem to fail; their cause triumphs, but their own overthrow is the price paid for the success of their cause. When was it that this conflict, and this character and issue of it, have not been fulfilled? So it was in the beginning. Cain, for instance, was envious of his brother Abel, and slew

him.   Enoch walked with God, and was a preacher of
righteousness, and God took him.   Ishmael mocked at
Isaac; Esau was full of wrath with Jacob, and resolved
to kill him.   Joseph's brethren were filled with bitter
hatred of him, debated about killing him, cast him into
a pit, and at last sold him into Egypt.   Afterwards,
in like manner, Korah, Dathan, and Abiram rose up
against Moses.   And, later still, Saul persecuted David;
and Ahab and Jezebel, Elijah; and the priests and the
prophets the Prophet Jeremiah.   Lastly, not to dwell
on other instances, the chief priests and Pharisees, full
of envy, rose up against our Lord Jesus Christ, and
delivered Him to the heathen governor, Pontius Pilate,
to be crucified.   So the Apostles, after Him, and especially St. Paul, were persecuted by their fierce and re-
vengeful countrymen : and from the way in which St.
Paul speaks on the subject we may infer that it is ever so
to be : "All that will live godly in Christ Jesus shall
suffer persecution :" or, as he says, after referring to the
history of Isaac and Ishmael, "As then he that was
born after the flesh persecuted him that was born after
the Spirit, even so it is now :" and indeed we see this
fulfilled in its measure before our eyes even at this day.
Hence our Saviour, to console all who suffer for His
sake, graciously says, "Blessed are they which are
persecuted for righteousness' sake, for theirs is the
kingdom of heaven [1]."

[1] 2 Tim. iii. 12.   Gal. iv. 29.   Matt. v. 10.

The case seems to be this :—those who do not serve God with a single heart, know they ought to do so, and they do not like to be reminded that they ought. And when they fall in with any one who does live to God, he serves to remind them of it, and that is unpleasant to them, and that is the first reason why they are angry with a religious man; the sight of him disturbs them and makes them uneasy.

And, in the next place, they feel in their hearts that he is in much better case than they are. They cannot help wishing—though they are hardly conscious of their own wish—they cannot help wishing that they were like him ; yet they have no intention of imitating him, and this makes them jealous and envious. Instead of being angry with themselves they are angry with him.

These are their first feelings : what follows? next they are very much tempted to deny that he *is* religious. They wish to get the thought of him out of their minds. Nothing would so relieve their minds as to find that there were no religious persons in the world, none better than themselves. Accordingly, they do all they can to believe that he is making a pretence of religion; they do their utmost to find out what looks like inconsistency in him. They call him a hypocrite and other names. And all this, if the truth must be spoken, because they hate the things of God, and therefore they hate His servants.

Accordingly, as far as they have power to do it, they persecute him, either, as the text implies, with cruel untrue words, or with cold, or fierce, or jealous looks, or in some worse ways. A good man is an offence to a bad man. The sight of him is a sort of insult; and he is irritated at him, and does him what harm he can. Thus Christians, in former times, were put to death by the heathen. As righteous Abel by Cain, as our Lord Jesus Christ, the Son of God, by the Jews, as St. Paul too by the heathen; so, many after him were put to death also, and that by the most cruel torments. It would not be right to describe the horrible inflictions which the children of God once endured at the hands of the children of the flesh; but we have some allusion to what had taken place in an earlier age, in a passage from St. Paul's Epistle to the Hebrews, from which you may judge of the more cruel trials which Christians afterwards endured. They " had trial of cruel mockings and scourgings, yea, moreover of bonds and imprisonment: they were stoned, they were sawn asunder, were tempted, were slain with the sword: they wandered about in sheep-skins and goat-skins; being destitute, afflicted, tormented; (of whom the world was not worthy:) they wandered in deserts, and in mountains, and in dens and caves of the earth [1]."

Praised be God, we live in times when this cannot take place! Hitherto, at least, He has guarded us in a

[1] Heb. xi. 36—38.

wonderful way. If any bad man did any serious harm to a religious man, he knows he would incur some punishment from the law of the land. Religious persons are protected in this day from all great persecutions, and they cannot sufficiently be thankful for it. The utmost they can suffer from the world is light indeed compared with what men suffered of old time. Yet St. Paul calls even his and their sufferings " our light affliction ;" and if their suffering was but light, compared with the glory which was to follow after death, much more is ours light, who cannot undergo persecution, if we would, and at best can only suffer very slight inconveniences from serving God faithfully.

And yet, nevertheless, most true is it, that even now, no one can give his mind to God, and show by his actions that he fears God, but he will incur the dislike and opposition of the world; and it is important he should be aware of this, and be prepared for it. He must not mind it, he must bear it, and in time (if God so will) he will overcome it.

There are a number of lesser ways in which careless ungodly persons may annoy and inconvenience those who desire to do their duty humbly and fully. Such, especially, are those, which seem intended in the text, unkind censure, carping, slander, ridicule, cold looks, rude language, insult, and, in some cases, oppression and tyranny. Whoever, therefore, sets about a religious life, must be prepared for these,—must be thankful if they

[VIII]   L

do not befall him; but must not be put out, must not think it a strange thing, if they do.

Now, my brethren, observe this; in bidding you endure reproach for Christ's sake, I am bidding you nothing which, as a minister of Christ, I do not wish to practise myself. Nay, it is what all ministers of Christ are obliged to practise; for, in all ages, *who* do you think it is that the world will first attack and oppose? Christ's ministers, of course. Who is there who can possibly so offend this bad world, as they whose very office is to remind the world of God and heaven? If all serious persons are disliked by the world, because they bring before it unpleasant truths, which it would fain forget if it could, this trial surely applies still more to those whose very profession and business it is to remind men of the truths of religion. A religious man does not intend to remind his neighbours; he goes on his own way; but they see him and cannot help being reminded. They see that he is well-conducted, and sober-minded, and reverent, and conscientious; that he never runs into any excess; that he never uses bad language; that he is regular at his prayers, regular at Church, regular at the most Holy Sacrament; they see all this, and, whether he will or no, they *are* reminded of their duty, and, as disliking to be reminded, they dislike him who reminds them. But if this be so in the case of common men, who wish to go on in a religious way without making any profession, how do you think it will fare with us, Christ's ministers, whose very duty it is to make a profession? Every thing about a clergyman is a warning to men, or ought to be, of the next world, of death and judgment, heaven and hell. His very dress is a memento. He does not dress like other men. His habits are a memento. His mode of speech is graver than that of others. His duties too are a memento. He is seen in Church reading prayers, baptizing, preaching; or he is seen teaching children; he is seen in works of charity; or he is seen studying. His life is given to objects out of sight. All that he does is intended to remind men that time is short, death is certain, and eternity long. And, this being so, do you think that men, being as they mostly are, careless and irreligious, do you think they like this? No; and still less, when he goes on to tell men of their errors and faults, and, as far as he can, to restrain them. And so in all ages you will find that the world has resisted and done its utmost to get rid of the preachers of repentance and holiness. It would stone Moses, it cast Daniel into the den of lions, and the three Children into the fiery furnace: St. Paul it beheaded, St. Peter it crucified, others it burnt, others it tortured even to death. And so it went on for many generations. But at last, as I said just now, religious persons have by degrees been sheltered by the law of the land from persecution, and Christ's ministers among them. And the world has got more humane and generous, if not more religious; and

God is sovereign over all. But though the devil cannot persecute us, he does what he can to oppose us. Surely this is so; for no one can look into the many publications of the day, without having proof of it; no one can go into places where persons meet together for refreshment, or for recreation, without hearing it; no one can travel on the road, without at times being witness to it. Christ's ministers are called names, untruths are told of them, they are ridiculed; and men encourage each other to oppose them, and to deceive them. And why? for this simple short reason, because they are God's messengers; and men in general do not like to be told of God. They say that they could do well enough without ministers of Christ; which really means, that they wish to do without God in the world.

Such is the portion to which all we, ministers of Christ, are called by our profession; and therefore, when we bid you prepare for the opposition of the world, we are calling you to nothing which we do not bear ourselves. It were well, could we, in all things, do first what we bid *you* do. There is no temptation or trial which you have, which in its kind we may not have to endure, or at least would not wish to endure, so far as it is lawful to wish it. St. Paul said to certain heathens, " We also are men of like passions with you[1]." St. Paul, and the Apostles, and all Christ's ministers after them, are of one nature with other men. They have to

[1] Acts xiv. 15.

go through what other men go through. They suffer pain, sorrow, bereavement, anxiety, desolateness, privations; and they have need, as other men, of patience, cheerfulness, faith, hope, contentment, resignation, firmness, to bear all that comes on them well. But even more than other men are they called on to bear the opposition of the world. They have to bear being ridiculed, slandered, ill-treated, overreached, disliked. All this is not pleasant to them naturally, any more than to other people. But they find it must be so; they cannot alter it; and they learn resignation and patience. This patience and resignation then I exhort you to cherish, my brethren, when the world scorns you for your religion; and withal cheerfulness and meekness, that you may bear your cross lightly, and not gloomily, or sadly, or complainingly.

For instance, persons may press you to do something which you know to be wrong—to tell an untruth, or to do what is not quite honest, or to go to companies whither you should not go; and they may show that they are vexed at the notion of your not complying. Still you must not comply. You must not do what you feel to be wrong, though you should thereby displease even those whom you would most wish to please.

Again: you must not be surprised, should you find that you are called a hypocrite, and other hard names; you must not mind it.

Again: you may be jeered at and mocked by your

acquaintance, for being strict and religious, for carefully coming to Church, keeping from bad language, and the like : you must not care for it.

Again, you may, perhaps, discover to your great vexation, that untruths are told of you by careless persons behind your backs, that what you do has been misrepresented, and that in consequence a number of evil things are believed about you by the world at large. Hard though it be, you must not care for it; remembering that more untruths were told of our Saviour and His Apostles than can possibly be told of you.

Again : you may find that not only the common run of men believe what is said against you, but even those with whom you wish to stand well. But if this happens through your conscientiousness you must not mind it, but must be cheerful, leaving your case in the hand of God, and knowing that He will bring it out into the light one day or another, in His own good time.

Again : persons may try to threaten or frighten you into doing something wrong, but you must not mind that; you must be firm.

In many, very many ways you may be called upon to bear the ill-usage of the world, or to withstand its attempts to draw you from God; but you must be firm, and you must not be surprised that they should be made. You must consider that it is your very calling to bear and to withstand. This is what you offer to God as a sort of return for His great mercies to you.

Did not Christ go through much more for you than you can possibly be called upon to undergo for Him? Did He bear the bitter cross who was sinless, and do you, who are at best so sinful, scruple to bear such poor trials and petty inconveniences?

In conclusion, I will but call your attention to two points, to which what I have said leads me.

First; Do not be too eager to suppose you are ill-treated for your religion's sake. Make as light of matters as you can. And beware of being severe on those who lead careless lives, or whom you think or know to be ill-treating you. Do not dwell on such matters. Turn your mind away from them. Avoid all gloominess. Be kind and gentle to those who are perverse, and you will very often, please God, gain them over. You should pray for those who lead careless lives, and especially if they are unkind to you. Who knows but God may hear your prayers, and turn their hearts, and bring them over to you? Do every thing for them but imitate them and yield to them. This is the true Christian spirit, to be meek and gentle under ill-usage, cheerful under slander, forgiving towards enemies, and silent in the midst of angry tongues.

Secondly, I would say, recollect you cannot do any one thing of all the duties I have been speaking of, without God's help. Any one who attempts to resist the world, or to do other good things by his own strength, will be sure to fall. We *can* do good things, but it is when God gives us power to do them. There-fore we must pray to Him for the power. When we are brought into temptation of any kind, we should lift up our hearts to God. We should say to Him, "Good Lord, deliver us." Our Lord, when He was going away, promised to His disciples a Comforter instead of Himself; that was God the Holy Ghost, who is still among us (though we see Him not), as Christ was with the Apostles. He has come in order to enlighten us, to guide us in the right way, and in the end to bring us to Christ in heaven. And He came down, as His name "Comforter" shows, especially to stand by, and com-fort, and strengthen those who are in any trouble, par-ticularly trouble from irreligious men. The disciples, when Christ went, had to go through much trouble, and therefore He comforted them by the coming of the Holy and Eternal Spirit, the Third Person in the Blessed Trinity. "These things I have spoken unto you," He says, "that in Me ye might have peace; in the world ye shall have tribulation, but be of good cheer, I have overcome the world [1]." When, then, religious persons are in low spirits, or are any way grieved at the difficul-ties which the world puts in their way, when they earnestly desire to do their duty, yet feel how weak they are, let them recollect that they are "not their own," but "bought with a price," and the dwelling-places and temples of the All-gracious Spirit.

[1] John xvi. 33.

Lastly; I am quite sure that none of us, even the best, have resisted the world as we ought to have done. Our faces have not been like flints; we have been afraid of men's words, and dismayed at their looks, and we have yielded to them at times against our better judgment. We have fancied, forsooth, the world could do us some harm while we kept to the commandments of God. Let us search our consciences; let us look back on our past lives. Let us try to purify and cleanse our hearts in God's sight. Let us try to live more like Christians, more like children of God. Let us earnestly beg of God to teach us more simply and clearly what our duty is. Let us beg of Him to give us the heart to love Him, and true repentance for what is past. Let us beg Him to teach us *how* to confess Him before men; lest if we deny Him now, He may deny us before the Angels of God hereafter.

SERMON XI.

Doing Glory to God in Pursuits of the World.

"Whether, therefore, ye eat or drink, or whatsoever ye do, do all to the glory of God."—I COR. X. 31.

WHEN persons are convinced that life is short, that it is unequal to any great purpose, that it does not display adequately, or bring to perfection the true Christian, when they feel that the next life is all in all, and that eternity is the only subject that really can claim or can fill their thoughts, then they are apt to undervalue this life altogether, and to forget its real importance. They are apt to wish to spend the time of their sojourning here in a positive separation from active and social duties: yet it should be recollected that the employments of this world, though not themselves heavenly, are, after all, the way to heaven—though not the fruit, are the seed of immortality—and are valuable, though not in themselves, yet for that to which they lead: but it is difficult to realize this. It is difficult to realize both truths at once, and to connect both truths together; steadily to contemplate the life to come, yet to act in this. Those who meditate, are likely to neglect those active duties which are, in fact, incumbent on them, and to dwell upon the thought of God's glory, till they forget to act to His glory. This state of mind is chided in figure in the words of the holy Angels to the Apostles, when they say, "Ye men of Galilee, why stand ye gazing up into heaven [1]?"

In various ways does the thought of the next world lead men to neglect their duty in this; and whenever it does so we may be sure that there is something wrong and unchristian, not in their thinking of the next world, but in their manner of thinking of it. For though the contemplation of God's glory may in certain times and persons allowably interfere with the active employments of life, as in the case of the Apostles when our Saviour ascended, and though such contemplation is even freely allowed or commanded us at certain times of each day; yet that is not a real and true meditation on Christ, but some counterfeit, which makes us dream away our time, or become habitually indolent, or which withdraws us from our existing duties, or unsettles us.

Yet the thought of the world unseen is apt to do so in various ways, and the worst way of all is when we have taken up a notion that it *ought* to do so. And indeed this is a temptation to which persons who desire to be religious are exposed in one shape or another in

[1] Acts i. 11.

every age, and in this age as well as in times past.
Men come to fancy that to lose taste and patience for
the businesses of this life is renouncing the world and
becoming spiritually-minded. We will say a person
has been thoughtless and irreligious; perhaps openly
so; or at least careless about religion, and though innocent of any flagrant sin, yet a follower of his own
will and fancy, and unpractised in any regular and
consistent course of religion. He has, perhaps, been
outwardly respectful to sacred things and persons, but
has had no serious thoughts about the next world. He
has taken good and evil—religion and the world—as
they came, first one and then the other, without much
consideration. He has been fond of gaiety and amusements, or he has been deeply interested in some pursuit
or other of time and sense,—whether it be his own trade
or profession, or some of the studies and employments
now popular. He has fallen in with the ways of the
company in which he has found himself; has been profane with the profane; then, again, has had for a season
religious impressions, which in turn have worn away.
Thus he has lived, and something has then occurred
really to rouse him and give him what is called a serious
turn. Such a person, man or woman, young or old,
certainly does need to take a serious turn, does require
a change; and no one but must be very glad to hear
that a change has taken place, though at the same time
there may be changes not much better than the change

which happened to him, whose soul, in our Lord's language, was but "swept and garnished;" not really changed in a heavenly way, and having but the semblance of faith and holiness upon it.

Now the cases I am speaking of are somewhat like that which our Saviour seems to speak of in the passage referred to. When a man has been roused to serious resolutions, the chances are, that he fails to take up with the one and only narrow way which leads to life. The chances are that "then cometh the wicked one," and persuades him to choose some path short of the true one—easier and pleasanter than it. And *this* is the kind of course to which he is often seduced, as we frequently witness it; viz. to feel a sort of dislike and contempt for his ordinary worldly business as something beneath him. He knows he must have what Scripture calls a spiritual mind, and he fancies that to have a spiritual mind it is absolutely necessary to renounce all earnestness or activity in his worldly employments, to profess to take no interest in them, to despise the natural and ordinary pleasures of life, violating the customs of society, adopting a melancholy air and a sad tone of voice, and remaining silent and absent when among his natural friends and relatives, as if saying to himself, "I have much higher thoughts than to engage in all these perishing miserable things;" acting with constraint and difficulty in the things about him; making efforts to turn things which occur to the purpose of what he considers spiritual reflection; using certain Scripture phrases and expressions; delighting to exchange Scripture sentiments with persons whom he meets of his own way of thinking; nay, making visible and audible signs of deep feeling when Scripture or other religious subjects are mentioned, and the like. He thinks he lives out of the world, and out of its engagements, if he shuts (as it were) his eyes, and sits down doing nothing. Altogether he looks upon his worldly occupation simply as a burden and a cross, and considers it all gain to be able to throw it off; and the sooner he can release himself from it, and the oftener, so much the better.

Now I am far from denying that a man's worldly occupation *may* be his cross. Again, I am far from denying that under circumstances it may be right even to retire from the world. But I am speaking of cases when it is a person's duty to remain in his worldly calling, and when he does remain in it, but when he cherishes dissatisfaction with it : whereas what he ought to feel is this,—that *while* in it he is to glorify God, not *out* of it, but *in* it, and *by means* of it, according to the Apostle's direction, "not slothful in business, fervent in spirit, serving the Lord." The Lord Jesus Christ our Saviour is best served, and with the most fervent spirit, when men are not slothful in business, but do their duty in that state of life in which it has pleased God to call them.

Now what leads such a person into this mistake is, that he sees that most men who engage cheerfully and diligently in worldly business, do so from a worldly spirit, from a low carnal love of the world; and so he thinks it is *his* duty, on the contrary, *not* to take a cheerful part in the world's business at all. And it cannot be denied that the greater part of the world is *absorbed* in the world; so much so that I am almost afraid to speak of the duty of being active in our worldly business, lest I should seem to give countenance to that miserable devotion to the things of time and sense, that love of bustle and management, that desire of gain, and that aiming at influence and importance, which abound on all sides. Bad as it is to be languid and indifferent in our secular duties, and to account this religion, yet it is far worse to be the slaves of this world, and to have our hearts in the concerns of this world. I do not know any thing more dreadful than a state of mind which is, perhaps, the characteristic of this country, and which the prosperity of this country so miserably fosters. I mean that ambitious spirit, to use a great word, but I know no other word to express my meaning—that low ambition which sets every one on the look-out to succeed and to rise in life, to amass money, to gain power, to depress his rivals, to triumph over his hitherto superiors, to affect a consequence and a gentility which he had not before, to affect to have an opinion on high subjects, to pretend to form a judgment upon sacred things, to choose his religion, to approve and condemn according to his taste, to become a partizan in extensive measures for the supposed temporal benefit of the community, to indulge the vision of great things which are to come, great improvements, great wonders: all things vast, all things new,—this most fearfully earthly and grovelling spirit is likely, alas! to extend itself more and more among our countrymen,— an intense, sleepless, restless, never-wearied, never-satisfied, pursuit of Mammon in one shape or other, to the exclusion of all deep, all holy, all calm, all reverent thoughts. *This* is the spirit in which, more or less (according to their different tempers), men do commonly engage in concerns of this world; and I repeat it, better, far better, were it to retire from the world altogether than thus to engage in it—better with Elijah to fly to the desert, than to serve Baal and Ashtoreth in Jerusalem.

But the persons I speak of, as despising this world, are far removed from the spirit of Elijah. To flee from the world, or strenuously to resist it, implies an energy and strength of mind which they have not. They do neither one thing nor the other; they neither flee it, nor engage zealously in its concerns; but they remain in the midst of them, doing them in an indolent and negligent way, and think this is to be spiritually minded; or, as in other cases, they really take an interest in them, and yet speak as if they despised them.

But surely it is possible to " serve the Lord," yet not to be " slothful in business ;" not over devoted to it, but not to retire from it. We may do *all things* whatever we are about to God's glory; we may do all things *heartily*, as to the Lord, and not to man, being both active yet meditative; and now let me give some instances to show what I mean.

1. " Do all to the glory of God," says St. Paul, in the text; nay, " whether we eat or drink ;" so that it appears nothing is too slight or trivial to glorify Him in. We will suppose then, to take the case mentioned just now; we will suppose a man who has lately had more serious thoughts than he had before, and determines to live more religiously. In consequence of the turn his mind has taken he feels a distaste for his worldly occupation, whether he is in trade, or in any mechanical employment which allows little exercise of mind. He now feels he would rather be in some other business, though in itself his present occupation is quite lawful and pleasing to God. The ill-instructed man will at once get impatient and quit it; or if he does not quit it, at least he will be negligent and indolent in it. But the true penitent will say to himself, " No ; if it be an irksome employment, so much the more does it suit *me*. I deserve no better. I do not deserve to be fed even with husks. I am bound to afflict my soul for my past sins. If I were to go in sackcloth and ashes, if I were to live on bread and water, if I were to wash the feet of

M

the poor day by day, it would not be too great an humiliation; and the only reason I do not, is, that I have no call that way, it would look ostentatious. Gladly then will I hail an inconvenience which will try me without any one's knowing it. Far from repining, I will, through God's grace, go cheerfully about what I do not like. I will deny myself. I know that with His help what is in itself painful, will thus be pleasant as done towards Him. I know well that there is no pain but may be borne comfortably, by the thought of Him, and by His grace, and the strong determination of the will; nay, none but may soothe and solace me. Even the natural taste and smell may be made to like what they naturally dislike; even bitter medicine, which is nauseous to the palate, may by a resolute will become tolerable. Nay, even sufferings and torture, such as martyrs have borne, have before now been rejoiced in and embraced heartily from love to Christ. I then, a sinner, will take this light inconvenience in a generous way, pleased at the opportunity of disciplining myself, and with self-abasement, as needing a severe penitence. If there be parts in my occupation which I especially dislike, if it requires a good deal of moving about and I wish to be at home, or if it be sedentary and I wish to be in motion, or if it requires rising early and I like to rise late, or if it makes me solitary and I like to be with friends, all this unpleasant part, as far as is consistent with my health, and so that it is not likely to be a snare to me, I will choose by preference. Again, I see my religious views are a hindrance to me. I see persons are suspicious of me. I see that I offend people by my scrupulousness. I see that to get on in life requires far more devotion to my worldly business than I can give consistently with my duty to God, or without its becoming a temptation to me. I know that I ought not, and (please God) I will not, sacrifice my religion to it. My religious seasons and hours shall be my own. I will not countenance any of the worldly dealings and practices, the over-reaching ways, the sordid actions in which others indulge. And if I am thrown back in life thereby, if I make less gains or lose friends, and so come to be despised, and find others rise in the world while I remain where I was, hard though this be to bear, it is an humiliation which becomes me in requital for my sins, and in obedience to God; and a very slight one it is, merely to be deprived of worldly successes, or rather it is a gain. And this may be the manner in which Almighty God will make an opening for me, if it is His blessed will, to leave my present occupation. But leave it without a call from God, I certainly must not. On the contrary, I will work in it the more diligently, as far as higher duties allow me."

2. A second reason which will animate the Christian will be a desire of letting his light shine before men. He will aim at winning others by his own diligence and activity. He will say to himself, " My parents " or

"my master" or "employer shall never say of me,
Religion has spoiled him. They shall see me more active
and alive than before. I will be punctual and attentive,
and adorn the Gospel of God our Saviour. My companions shall never have occasion to laugh at any affecta-
tion of religious feeling in me. No; I will affect nothing.
In a manly way I will, with God's blessing, do my duty.
I will not, as far as I can help, dishonour His service by
any strangeness or extravagance of conduct, any un-
reality of words, any over-softness or constraint of
manner; but they shall see that the fear of God only
makes those who cherish it more respectable in the
world's eyes as well as more heavenly-minded. What a
blessed return it will be for God's mercies to me, if I,
who am like a brand plucked out of the burning, be
allowed, through His great mercy, to recommend that
Gospel to others which He has revealed to me, and to
recommend it, as on the one hand by my strictness in
attending God's ordinances, in discountenancing vice
and folly, and by a conscientious walk; so, on the other
hand, by all that is of good report in social life, by
uprightness, honesty, prudence, and straightforwardness,
by good temper, good-nature, and brotherly love!"

3. Thankfulness to Almighty God, nay, and the
inward life of the Spirit itself, will be additional principles causing the Christian to labour diligently in his
calling. He will see God in all things. He will
recollect our Saviour's life. Christ was brought up to

a humble trade. When he labours in his own, he will think of his Lord and Master in His. He will recollect that Christ went down to Nazareth and was subject to His parents, that He walked long journeys, that He bore the sun's heat and the storm, and had not where to lay His head. Again, he knows that the Apostles had various employments of this world before their calling; St. Andrew and St. Peter fishers, St. Matthew a tax-gatherer, and St. Paul, even after his calling, still a tent-maker. Accordingly, in whatever comes upon him, he will endeavour to discern and gaze (as it were) on the countenance of his Saviour. He will feel that the true contemplation of that Saviour lies *in* his worldly business; that as Christ is seen in the poor, and in the persecuted, and in children, so is He seen in the employments which He puts upon His chosen, whatever they be; that in attending to his own calling he will be meeting Christ; that if he neglect it, he will not on that account enjoy His presence at all the more, but that while performing it, he will see Christ revealed to his soul amid the ordinary actions of the day, as by a sort of sacrament. Thus he will take his worldly business as a gift from Him, and will love it as such.

4. True humility is another principle which will lead us to desire to glorify God in our worldly employments if possible, instead of resigning them. Christ evidently puts His greater blessings on those whom the world despises. He has bid His followers take the lowest

seat. He says that he who would be great must be as the servant of all, that he who humbleth himself shall be exalted; and He Himself washed His disciples' feet. Nay, He tells us, that He will gird Himself, and serve them who have watched for Him; an astonishing condescension, which makes us almost dumb with fear and rejoicing. All this has its effect upon the Christian, and he sets about his business with alacrity, and without a moment's delay, delighting to humble himself, and to have the opportunity of putting himself in that condition of life which our Lord especially blest.

5. Still further, he will use his worldly business as a means of keeping him from vain and unprofitable thoughts. One cause of the heart's devising evil is, that time is given it to do so. The man who has his daily duties, who lays out his time for them hour by hour, is saved a multitude of sins which have not time to get hold upon him. The brooding over insults received, or the longing after some good not granted, or regret at losses which have befallen us, or at the loss of friends by death, or the attacks of impure and shameful thoughts, these are kept off from him who takes care to be diligent and well employed. Leisure is the occasion of all evil. Idleness is the first step in the downward path which leads to hell. If we do not find employment to engage our minds with, Satan will be sure to find his own employment for them. Here we see the difference of motive with which a religious and a

worldly-minded man may do the same thing. Suppose a person has had some sad affliction, say a bereavement : men of this world, having no pleasure in religion, not liking to dwell on a loss to them irreparable, in order to drown reflection, betake themselves to worldly pursuits to divert their thoughts and banish gloom. The Christian under the same circumstances does the same thing; but it is from a fear lest he should relax and enfeeble his mind by barren sorrow; from a dread of becoming discontented; from a belief that he is pleasing God better, and is likely to secure his peace more fully, by not losing time; from a feeling that, far from forgetting those whom he has lost by thus acting, he shall only enjoy the thought of them the more really and the more religiously.

6. Lastly, we see what judgment to give in a question sometimes agitated, whether one should retire from our worldly business at the close of life, to give our thoughts more entirely to God. To wish to do so is so natural, that I suppose there is no one who would not wish it. A great many persons are not allowed the privilege, a great many are allowed it through increasing infirmities or extreme old age; but every one, I conceive, if allowed to choose, would think it a privilege to be allowed it, though a great many would find it difficult to determine *when* was the fit time. But let us consider what is the reason of this so natural a wish. I fear that it is often not a religious wish, often only

partially religious. I fear a great number of persons who aim at retiring from the world's business, do so under the notion of their then enjoying themselves somewhat after the manner of the rich man in the Gospel, who said, " Soul, thou hast much goods laid up for many years." If this is the predominant aim of any one, of course I need not say that it is a fatal sin, for Christ Himself has said so. Others there are who are actuated by a mixed feeling; they are aware that they do not give so much time to religion as they ought; they do not live by rule; nay, they are not satisfied with the correctness or uprightness of some of the practices or customs which their way of life requires of them, and they get tired of active business as life goes on, and wish to be at ease. So they look to their last years as a time of retirement, in which they may *both* enjoy themselves *and* prepare for heaven. And thus they satisfy both their conscience and their love of the world. At present religion is irksome to them; but then, as they hope, duty and pleasure will go together. Now, putting aside all other mistakes which such a frame of mind evidences, let it be observed, that if they are at present *not* serving God with all their hearts, but look forward to a time when they shall do so, then it is plain that, when at length they *do* put aside worldly cares and turn to God, if ever they do, that time must necessarily be a time of deep humiliation, if it is to be acceptable to Him, not a comfortable retirement. Who ever heard of a pleasurable, easy, joyous repentance? It is a contradiction in terms. These men, if they do but reflect a moment, must confess that their present mode of life, supposing it be not so strict as it should be, is heaping up tears and groans for their last years, not enjoyment. The longer they live as they do at present, not only the more unlikely is it that they will repent at all; but even if they do, the more bitter, the more painful must their repentance be. The only way to escape suffering for sin hereafter is to suffer for it here. Sorrow here or misery hereafter; they cannot escape one or the other.

Not for any worldly reason, then, not on any presumptuous or unbelieving motive, does the Christian desire leisure and retirement for his last years. Nay, he will be content to do without these blessings, and the highest Christian of all is he whose heart is so stayed on God, that he does not wish or need it; whose heart is so set on things above, that things below as little excite, agitate, unsettle, distress, and seduce him, as they stop the course of nature, as they stop the sun and moon, or change summer and winter. Such were the Apostles, who, as the heavenly bodies, went out " to all lands," full of business, and yet full too of sweet harmony, even to the ends of the earth. Their calling was heavenly, but their work was earthly; they were in labour and trouble till the last; yet consider how calmly St. Paul and St. Peter write in their last days.

St. John, on the other hand, was allowed in a great measure, to retire from the cares of his pastoral charge, and such, I say, will be the natural wish of every religious man, whether his ministry be spiritual or secular; but, not in order to *begin* to fix his mind on God, but merely because, though he may contemplate God as truly and be as holy in heart in active business as in quiet, still it is more becoming and suitable to meet the stroke of death (if it be allowed us) silently, collectedly, solemnly, than in a crowd and a tumult. And hence it is, among other reasons, that we pray in the Litany to be delivered "from *sudden* death."

On the whole, then, what I have said comes to this, that whereas Adam was sentenced to labour as a punishment, Christ has by His coming sanctified it as a means of grace and a sacrifice of thanksgiving, a sacrifice cheerfully to be offered up to the Father in His name.

It is very easy to speak and teach this, difficult to do it; very difficult to steer between the two evils,—to use this world as not abusing it, to be active and diligent in this world's affairs, yet not for this world's sake, but for God's sake. It requires the greater effort for a minister of Christ to speak of it, for this reason; because he is not called upon in the same sense in which others are to practise the duty. He is not called, as his people are, to the professions, the pursuits, and cares of this world; his work is heavenly, and to it he gives himself wholly. It is a work which, we trust, is not likely to carry him off from God; not only because it is His work, but, what is a more sure reason, because commonly it gains no great thanks from men. However, for this reason it is difficult for Christian ministers to speak about your trial in this matter, my brethren, because it is not theirs. We are tried by the command to live out of the world, and you by the command to live in it.

May God give us grace in our several spheres and stations to do His will and adorn His doctrine; that whether we eat and drink, or fast and pray, labour with our hands or with our minds, journey about or remain at rest, we may glorify Him who has purchased us with His own blood!

SERMON XII.

Vanity of Human Glory.

"The world knoweth us not, because it knew Him not."—1 JOHN iii. 1.

OF St. Simon and St. Jude, the Saints whom we this day commemorate, little is known[1]. St. Jude, indeed, still lives in the Church in his Catholic epistle; but of his history we only know that he was brother to St. James the Less, and nearly related to our Lord; and that, like St. Peter, he had been a married man. Besides his name of Jude or Judas, he is also called Thaddæus and Lebbæus in the Gospels. Of St. Simon we only know that he was called the Canaanite, or Zealot, for the words have the same meaning, belonging, before his conversion, to a certain fierce sect, who, under the idea they were doing God service, took upon themselves to execute the law upon offenders without legal authority, and without formal accusation or trial. It is said that both Apostles were at length martyred

[1] Preached on the Festival of St. Simon and St. Jude.

in the course of their efforts to gather together God's elect into His fold.

Little is known of St. Simon and St. Jude; they laboured and they taught in their generation; they were gifted with miraculous powers, and by their preaching founded churches and saved souls; they travelled into the East and West, till at last they were taken away from the earth. Yet we know little of their history now. Although "honoured in their generation, and the glory of their times," yet they "have no memorial, but are perished as though they had never been[1]." St. Jude's Epistle, indeed, is a standing monument, yet not of his doings, but of his gifts. What he wrote leads us to conjecture indeed what he was; but of his history, we know no more than of that of St. Simon.

And hence we draw an important lesson for ourselves, which, however obvious, is continually forgotten by us in the actual business of life; viz. to do our duty without aiming at the world's praise. Mankind knows nothing of St. Simon's and St. Jude's deeds and sufferings, though these were great; yet there is One who "knows their works, and labour, and patience, . . . and how they bore . . . and for His Name's sake laboured, and fainted not[2]." Their deeds are blotted out from history, but not from the Lamb's book of life; for "blessed are they who die in Him, . . . that they

---

[1] Ecclus. xliv. 7. 9.   [2] Rev. ii. 2, 3.

may rest from their labours; and their works do follow
them [1]."

On this great practical rule, viz. to do what we do
heartily, as unto the Lord, and not unto men, I shall
now make some remarks; and in doing so, I shall be
pointing out a mode in which we may follow these
blessed Saints, whose lives at first sight seem to have
left no pattern behind them for our imitation.

In heathen times, when men understood that they
had souls, yet did not know what was the soul's true
happiness, or how it was to be gained, much was
thought, and more talked, of what they called *glory,
fame, honour.* This was natural, as a little consideration will show. For before men begin to exercise
their minds, while they remain ignorant and dull, the
common pleasures of sense satisfy them—eating, drink-
ing, and making merry. They do not think of the
morrow. They have no end in view, and act on no
plan. But when intelligence is awakened, and they
learn to feel, reflect, hope, plan, and exert themselves;
then mere animal indulgences are not enough for them,
and they look about for some higher pleasures, more
lasting and more refined. This is the real effect of that
civilization which is so much extolled; it gives men
refined wishes, and sets them on gratifying them. An
enlightened age is one which feels the wants of human
nature. Knowledge and mental cultivation render men

[1] Rev. xiv. 13.

alive to the things around them, busy, and restless; but
they do no more than make men sensible of their wants;
they find no remedy for them; they bring no appro-
priate food to the hunger they create : for it is religion
alone can do this.

Now the ancient heathen whom I speak of were just
in this state; having minds cultivated and refined in-
tellectually, they felt the capabilities of man for acting
on a large field, and the need of some stimulus to make
him act thus. They saw that human nature was capable of great things, and they perceived that some great
goods must be attainable in some way or other, though
they did not well know what they were. Feelings such
as these, acting upon men in the tumult of life, with
their passions awake, keenly set on (what are called)
political objects, and averse to those self-denying habits
which conscience (if listened to) would have suggested
to be the way to that unknown happiness which their
heart was imagining, led them to think of what they
called glory and popularity as the greatest of goods,
and that to which they ought especially to aspire.

Now what exactly they wished to signify by the word
" glory," is difficult to say, for they were apt to speak
of it as if it were some real thing, and that, too, which
one could possess and make one's own; yet, if we
come to consider its real meaning, it plainly stands for
nothing else than the praise of other men, the being
admired, honoured, and feared; or, more commonly,

having a celebrated *name;* that is, for a something external to ourselves. But whatever precise notions they wished to attach to the word, they used to talk in glowing language of the necessity of going through dangers and sufferings for glory's sake,—labouring to benefit the world for glory,—and dying for glory.

Now when we read of poor heathens using this language, it is our duty to pity them, for it is plain enough to any sober reasoner, that nothing is so vain as to talk of this glory being a real and substantial good; for there is no better reason for my being happy because my name is celebrated, than because any thing else is celebrated which, accidentally, and for a time, is connected with myself, and called mine. My name is my own only in the case of those who use it in speaking of me; i. e. of those who happen to see and know me. But when those who never saw me talk much of my name, they do me no more good or harm than if they celebrated any thing else which *I* may know to be mine. They may praise a house that was once mine—that is not praising me; nor, in like manner, is it doing me any good, or honouring me, when those who never saw me use my name respectfully. It is a mere imagination, which can give no solid or lasting pleasure. There is some meaning and sense (though great wickedness) in coveting our neighbour's house or garden, horse or ass; the unjust steward, though a bad man, at least acted wisely, i. e. according to a worldly wisdom; but those who covet honour, I mean a great name, really covet no substantial thing at all, and are not only " the most offending men alive," inasmuch as this passion for fame may carry them on to the most atrocious crimes, but also the most foolish of men.

Now, in the ancient heathen we may blame, but we must pity this sin, because it at least evidenced in them a knowledge of a great want of human nature, and was so far the sign of a higher state of mind than that of others who did not feel any wants at all, who had no notion of any but selfish enjoyments, and were content to live and die like the brutes that perish. Their sin lay, not in being anxious for some good or other, which was not before their eyes, but in not consulting their own hearts on the subject, and going the way which their conscience told them. But, I say, they were heathens,—they had no Bible, no Church; and therefore we pity them; and by their errors are reminded to look to ourselves, and see how far we are clean from their sin.

Now it is a most melancholy fact, that Christians are chargeable, for all their light, with the same foolish irrational sin. This was not at first sight to be expected. This is a peculiar case. Observe; I do not say it is wonderful that we should seek the praise of persons we know. This I can understand. We all naturally love to be respected and admired, and in due limits perhaps we may be allowed to do so; the love of praise

is capable of receiving a religious discipline and character. But the surprising thing is, that we should leave
the thought of present goods, whether sensual enjoyments, or the more refined pleasure which the praise
of our friends brings us, yet without going on to seek
the good of the next world; that we should deny ourselves, yet not deny ourselves for a reality, but for a
shadow. It is natural, I say, to love to have deference
and respect paid us by our acquaintance; but I am
speaking of the desire of glory, that is, the praise of a
vast multitude of persons we never saw, or shall see, or
care about; and this, I say, is a depraved appetite, the
artificial produce of a falsely enlightened intellect; as
unmeaning as it is sinful, or rather more sinful, because
it is so very unmeaning; excusable indeed in heathen,
not only because they knew no better, but because they
had no better good clearly proposed to them; but in
Christians, who have the favour of God and eternal life
set before them, deeply criminal, turning away, as they
do, from the bread of heaven, to feed upon ashes, with
a deceived and corrupted imagination.

This love of indiscriminate praise, then, is an odious,
superfluous, wanton sin, and we should put it away with
a manly hatred, as something irrational and degrading.
Shall man, born for high ends, the servant and son of
God, the redeemed of Christ, the heir of immortality, go
out of his way to have his mere name praised by a
vast populace, or by various people, of whom he knows

nothing, and most of whom (if he saw them) he would himself be the first to condemn? It is odious; yet young persons of high minds and vigorous powers, are especially liable to be led captive by this snare of the devil. If reasoning does not convince them, let facts,— the love of glory has its peculiar condemnation in its consequences. No sin has been so productive of wide-spread enduring ruin among mankind: wars and con-quests are the means by which men have most reckoned on securing it. A tree is known by its fruit.

These remarks apply to the love of indiscriminate praise in all its shapes. Few persons, indeed, are in a condition to be tempted by the love of glory; but all persons may be tempted to indulge in vanity, which is nothing else but the love of general admiration. A vain person is one who likes to be praised, whoever is the praiser, whether good or bad. Now consider, how few men are not in their measure vain, till they reach that period of life when by the course of nature vanity disappears? Let all Christians carefully ask themselves, whether they are not very fond, not merely of the praise of their superiors and friends—this is right,—but of that of any person, any chance-comer, about whom they know nothing. Who is not open to flattery? and if he seems not to be exposed to it, is it not that he is too shrewd or too refined to be beguiled by any but what is delicate and unostentatious? A man never considers who it is who praises him. But the most dangerous, perhaps, of all kinds of vanity is to be vain of our personal appearance; most dangerous, for such persons are ever under temptation—I may say, ever sinning. Wherever they go they carry their snare with them; and their idle love of admiration is gratified without effort by the very looks of those who gaze upon them.

Now I shall say something upon the natural and rational love of praise, and how far it may be safely indulged. As I have already said, it is *natural* to desire the esteem of all those with whom we have intercourse, all whom we love. Indeed, Almighty God intends us to do so. When we love a person, we cannot but wish he should love us; but he cannot love us, without also feeling respect and esteem towards us. And as to the question, from whom we should desire praise, and how far, we have this simple rule—from all who stand to us in Christ's place. Christ Himself is our great Judge; from Him we must supremely seek praise; and as far as men are in His place, so far may we seek it from men. We may desire the praise of our parents and superiors, and the praise of good men— in a word, all whom we have a value for; but the desire of indiscriminate praise, the praise of those for whom we have no respect or regard, this is the mischief. We *may* desire the praise of those we have never seen, if we believe them to be good men. St. Paul not only speaks of the mutual rejoicing between himself and the

Corinthians[1], who knew each other, but likewise returns thanks that the fame of the faith of the Romans was spread all over the Christian world[2]. And in this way we may desire the praise of good persons yet unborn— I mean the Church of God, to the end of time. St. Mary, in the hymn we daily use, returns thanks that "from henceforth all generations shall call her blessed[3]." But this feeling of hers is very different from the desire of what is called glory, posthumous fame, fame after death; as if, forsooth, it were a great thing to have one's name familiar to the mouths of the mixed multitude of this world, of swearers, and jesters, and liars, and railers, and blasphemers, and of all those men, who even if they do not sin grossly in deed, yet use their tongues for evil, speak the words of the world, slander the Church, speak evil of dignities, propagate error, and defend sinners; a great thing truly, and much to be desired, to be honoured by that evil world which dishonours God and His Son!

One additional caution I must add, about allowing ourselves the praise of others; not only must we desire the praise of none but good men, but we must not earnestly desire to be known even by many good men. The truth is, we cannot know, really know, many persons at all, and it is always dangerous to delight in the praises of strangers, even though we believe them to be good men, and much more to seek their praises, which is

[1] 2 Cor. i. 4   [2] Rom. i. 8.   [3] Luke i. 48.

a kind of ambition.   And further than this, it is more agreeable to the Christian temper to be satisfied rather to know and to be known by a few, and to grow day by day in their esteem and affection, than to desire one's name to be on the lips of many, though they profess religion, and associate us with religious objects.   And it is our great privilege to have the real blessing in our power, while the fancied good alone is difficult to be gained.   Few Christians can be great or can leave a name to posterity; but most Christians will, in the length of their lives, be able to secure the love and praise of one or two, who are to them the representatives of Him whom "having not seen they love," and in whose presence, or at least in whose memory, they may comfort their heart till He come.   This doubtless has been the happiness of many saints who have not even left their names behind them.   It was the privilege doubtless of St. Simon and St. Jude.   They, indeed, were not simply unknown to the world in their life-time, but even hated and persecuted by it.   Upon them came our Saviour's prophecy, that "men should revile them . . . . and say all manner of evil against them falsely for His sake[1]."   Yet in the affection the Church bore them, in the love they bore to each other, and, above all, the praise of that Saviour whom they had followed on earth, and who named them in the number of those who had continued with Him in His tempta-

[1] Matt. v. 11.

tions[1], and were written in heaven, they had a real glory, not as the world giveth. Who can estimate, who can imagine the deep, the wonderful, the awful joy which the approbation of Christ would impart to them? When we consider how intimately they were allowed to associate with Him, how they were witnesses of His heavenly conversation through the days of His flesh, of His acts of mercy, of His Divine words, of the grace, the tenderness, the sanctity, the majesty, the calmness, which reigned within Him; of His knowledge, His wisdom, His perfect love of God, His zeal for God's service, His patient obedience,—and much more when they knew the dread secret of what He was before He came on earth, what He was even while on earth in presence, —to have had a smile, an encouraging word, from Him, was it not a privilege to treasure in memory beyond any thing else, a remembrance so bright that every thing else looked discoloured and dim? and would it not have amounted to a loss of reason in them to have even had the thought of seeking the praise of weak, ignorant, sinful mortals?

Let us seek this praise which cometh of God, though we shall not have that sensible experience of it which the Apostles were vouchsafed. Let us seek it, for it is to be obtained; it is given to those worthy of it. The poorest, the oldest, and most infirm among us, those who are living not merely in obscurity, but are despised

[1] Luke xxii. 28—30.

and forgotten, who seem to answer no good purpose by living on, and whose death will not be felt even by their neighbours as a loss, these even may obtain our Saviour's approving look, and receive the future greeting, "Well done, good and faithful servant."

Go on, then, contentedly in the path of duty, seeking Christ in His house and in His ordinances, and He will be your glory at His coming. He will own you before His Father. Let the world record in history the names of heroes, statesmen, and conquerors, and reward courage, and ability, and skill, and perseverance, with its proud titles of honour. Verily, these have their reward. Your names will be written in Heaven, with those of St. Simon and St. Jude, and the other Apostles. You will have the favour of Him whose favour is life. "The secret of the Lord is with them that fear Him: and He will show them His covenant [1]."

[1] Ps. xxv. 14.

SERMON XIII.

Truth hidden when not sought after.

" They shall turn away their ears from the truth, and shall be turned unto fables."—2 TIM. iv. 4.

FROM these words of the blessed Apostle, written shortly before he suffered martyrdom, we learn, that there is such a thing as religious truth, and therefore there is such a thing as religious error. We learn that religious truth is *one*—and therefore that all views of religion *but* one are wrong. And we learn, moreover, that so it was to be (for his words are a prophecy) that professed Christians, forgetting this, should turn away their ears from the one Truth, and should be turned, not to one, but to many fables. All this is fulfilled before our eyes; our religious creeds and professions at this day are many; but Truth is one: therefore they cannot all be right, or rather almost all of them must be wrong. That is, the multitude of men are wrong, so far as they differ; and as they differ, not about trivial points, but about great matters, it follows that the multitude of men, whether by their own fault or not, are wrong even in the greater matters of religion.

This is a most solemn thought, and a perplexing one. However, there is another which, though it ought not to be perplexing, is perplexing still, and perhaps has greater need to be considered and explained; I mean that men of learning and ability are so often wrong in religious matters also. It is a stumbling-block to many, when they find that those who seem the legitimate guides furnished by God's providence, who are in some sense the natural prophets and expounders of the truth, that these too are on many sides, and therefore many of them on the side of error also. There are persons who can despise the opinions of the *many*, and feel that *they* are not right, but that truth, if it be to be found, lies with the *few ;* and since men of ability *are* among the few, they think that truth lies with men of ability, and when after all they are told that able men are ranged on contrary sides in religious questions, they either hastily deny the fact, or they are startled, and stagger in their faith.

But on the contrary, let us honestly confess what is certain, that not the ignorant, or weakminded, or dull, or enthusiastic, or. extravagant only turn their ears from the Truth and are turned unto fables, but also men of powerful minds, keen perceptions, extended views, ample and various knowledge. Let us, I say, confess it; yet let us not believe in the Truth the less on account of it.

I say that in the number of the adversaries of the Truth, there are many men of highly endowed and highly cultivated minds. Why should we deny this? It is unfair to do so; and not only unfair, but very unnecessary. What is called ability and talent does not make a man a Christian; nay, often, as may be shown without difficulty, it is the occasion of his rejecting Christianity, or this or that part of it. Not only in the higher ranks of society do we see this; even in the humble and secluded village, it will commonly be found, that those who have greater gifts of mind than others around them, who have more natural quickness, shrewdness, and wit, are the very persons who are the most likely to turn out ill—who are least under the influence of religious principles—and neither obey nor even revere the Gospel of salvation which Christ has brought us.

Now if we consult St. Paul's Epistles to the Corinthians, we shall find the same state of things existing even in the first age of Christianity. Even the Apostle speaks of those who were blind, or to whom his Gospel was hid; and he elsewhere describes them, not as the uneducated and dull of understanding, but as the wise of this world, the scribe and the disputer. Even then, before the Apostle's prophecy in the text was fulfilled, there were many who erred from the truth even in the midst of light, and in spite of superior intellectual endowments and acquirements.

Does not our Saviour Himself say the same thing, when He thanks His Father, Lord of heaven and earth, that He hath hid these things from the wise and prudent, and revealed them unto babes?

Now it should not surprise us when men of acute and powerful understandings more or less reject the Gospel, for this reason, that the Christian revelation addresses itself to our hearts, to our love of truth and goodness, our fear of sinning, and our desire to gain God's favour; and quickness, sagacity, depth of thought, strength of mind, power of comprehension, perception of the beautiful, power of language, and the like, though they are excellent gifts, are clearly quite of a different kind from these spiritual excellences—a man may have the one without having the other. *This,* then, is the plain reason why able, or again why learned men are so often defective Christians, because there is no necessary connexion between faith and ability; because faith is one thing and ability is another; because ability of mind is a *gift,* and faith is a *grace.* Who would ever argue that a man could, like Samson, conquer lions or throw down the gates of a city, because he was able, or accomplished, or experienced in the business of life? Who would ever argue that a man could see because he could hear, or run with the swift because he had "the tongue of the learned[1]"? These gifts are different in kind. In like manner, powers of mind and reli-

[1] Isa. l. 4.

gious principles and feelings are distinct gifts; and as all the highest spiritual excellence, humility, firmness, patience, would never enable a man to read an unknown tongue, or to enter into the depths of science, so all the most brilliant mental endowments, wit, or imagination, or penetration, or depth, will never of themselves make us wise in religion. And as we should fairly and justly deride the savage who wished to decide questions of science or literature by the sword, so may we justly look with amazement on the error of those who think that they can master the high mysteries of spiritual truth, and find their way to God, by what is commonly called reason, i. e. by the random and blind efforts of mere mental acuteness, and mere experience of the world.

That Truth, which St. Paul preached, addresses itself to our spiritual nature : it will be rightly understood, valued, accepted, by none but lovers of truth, virtue, purity, humility, and peace. Wisdom will be justified of her children. Those, indeed, who are thus endowed may and will go on to use their powers of mind, whatever they are, in the service of religion; none but they can use them aright. Those who reject revealed truth wilfully, are such as do not love moral and religious truth. It is bad men, proud men, men of hard hearts, and unhumbled tempers, and immoral lives, these are they who reject the Gospel. These are they of whom St. Paul speaks in another Epistle—" If our Gospel be hid, it is hid to them that are lost, in whom the god of this world hath blinded the minds of them which believe not." With this agree the instances of turning the ears from the truth which the New Testament affords us. Who were they who were the enemies of Christ and His Apostles? The infidel Sadducees, the immoral, hard-hearted, yet hypocritical Pharisees, Herod, who married his brother Philip's wife[1], and Felix, who trembled when St. Paul reasoned of righteousness, temperance, and judgment to come[2]. On the other hand, men of holy and consistent lives, as Cornelius the Centurion, and those who were frequenters of religious ordinances, as Simeon and Anna, these became Christians. So it is now. If men turn unto fables of their own will, they do it on account of their pride, or their love of indolence and self-indulgence.

This should be kept in mind when Christians are alarmed, as they sometimes are, on hearing instances of infidelity or heresy among those who read, reflect, and inquire; whereas, however we may mourn over such instances, we have no reason to be surprised at them. It is quite enough for Christians to be able to show, as they well can, that belief in revealed religion is not inconsistent with the highest gifts and acquirements of mind, that men even of the strongest and highest intellect have been Christians; but they have as little reason to be perplexed at finding *other* men of ability

[1] Matt. xiv. 3.　　　　　　　[2] Acts xxiv. 25.

not true believers, as at finding that certain *rich* men are not true believers, or certain *poor* men, or some in every rank and circumstance of life. A belief in Christianity has hardly more connexion with what is called talent, than it has with riches, station, power, or bodily strength.

Now let me explain what I have said by a further remark. Is it not plain that earnestness is necessary for gaining religious truth? On the other hand, is it not a natural effect of ability to save us trouble, and even to tempt us to dispense with it, and to lead us to be indolent? Do not we see this even in the case of children—the more clever are the more idle, because they rely on their own quickness and power of apprehension? Is indolence the way to gain knowledge from God? Yet this surely is continually forgotten in the world. It is forgotten in a measure even by the best of Christians, for no man on earth seeks to know God's will, and to do His duty with an earnestness suitable to the importance of the object. But not to speak thus rigorously, let us consider for an instant how eagerly men in general pursue objects of this world; now with what portion of this eagerness do they exert themselves to know the truth of God's word? Undeniable, then, as is the doctrine that God does not reveal Himself to those who do not seek Him, it is certain that its truth is not really felt by us, or we should seek Him more earnestly than we do.

Nothing is more common than to think that we shall gain religious knowledge as a thing of course, without express trouble on our part. Though there is no art or business of this world which is learned without time and exertion, yet it is commonly conceived that the knowledge of God and our duty will come as if by accident or by a natural process. Men go by their feelings and likings; they take up what is popular, or what comes first to hand. They think it much if they now and then have serious thoughts, if they now and then open the Bible; and their minds recur with satisfaction to such seasons, as if they had done some very great thing, never remembering that to seek and gain religious truth is a long and systematic work. And others think that education will do every thing for them, and that if they learn to read, and use religious words, they understand religion itself. And others again go so far as to maintain that exertion is *not* necessary for discovering the truth. They say that religious truth is simple and easily acquired; that Scripture, being intended for all, is at once open to all, and that if it had difficulties, that very circumstance would be an objection to it. And others, again, maintain that there *are* difficulties in religion, and that this shows that it is an indifferent matter whether they seek or not as to those matters which are difficult.

In these and other ways do men deceive themselves into a carelessness about religious truth. And is not all this varied negligence sufficient to account for the varieties of religious opinion which we see all around us? Do not these two facts just illustrate each other; the discordance of our religious opinions needing some explanation; and our actual indolence and negligence in seeking the truth accounting for it? How many sects, all professing Christianity, but opposed to each other, dishonour this country! Doubtless if men sought the truth with one tenth part of the zeal with which they seek to acquire wealth or secular knowledge, their differences would diminish year by year. Doubtless if they gave a half or a quarter of the time to prayer for Divine guidance which they give to amusement or recreation, or which they give to dispute and contention, they would ever be approximating to each other. We differ in opinion; therefore we cannot all be right; many must be wrong; many must be turned from the truth; and why is this, but on account of that undeniable fact which we see before us, that we do not pray and seek for the Truth?

But this melancholy diversity is sometimes explained, as I just now hinted, in another way. Some men will tell us that this difference of opinion in religious matters which exists, is a proof, not that the Truth is withheld from us on account of our negligence in seeking it, but that religious truth is not worth seeking at all, or that it is not given us. The present confused and perplexed state of things, which is really a proof of God's anger at our negligence, these men say is a proof that religious truth cannot be obtained; that there is no such thing as religious truth; that there is no right or wrong in religion; that, provided we *think* ourselves right, one set of opinions is as good as another; that we shall all come right in the end if we do but mean well, or rather if we do not mean ill. That is, we create confusion by our negligence and disobedience, and then excuse our negligence by the existence of that confusion. It is no uncommon thing, I say, for men to say, "that in religious matters God has willed that men should differ," and to support their opinion by no better argument than the fact that they *do* differ; and they go on to conclude that *therefore* we need not perplex ourselves about matters of *faith*, about which, after all, we cannot be certain. Others, again, in a similar spirit, argue that forms and ordinances are of no account; that they are little matters; that it is uncertain what is right and what is wrong in them, and that to insist on them as important to religion is the mark of a narrow mind. And others, again, it is to be feared, go so far as to think that indulgence of the passions, or self-will, or selfishness, or avarice, is not wrong, because it is the way of the world and cannot be prevented.

To all such arguments against religious truth, it is sufficient to reply, that no one who does not seek the truth with all his heart and strength, can tell what is

of importance and what is not; that to attempt carelessly to decide on points of faith or morals is a matter
of serious presumption; that no one knows *whither* he
will be carried *if* he seeks the Truth perseveringly, and
therefore, that since he cannot see at first starting the
course into which his inquiries will be divinely directed,
he *cannot* possibly say beforehand whether they may
not lead him on to certainty as to things which at
present he thinks trifling or extravagant or irrational.
" What I do," said our Lord to St. Peter, " thou
knowest not now, but thou shalt know hereafter."
" *Seek*, and ye shall find;" this is the Divine rule, " If
thou *criest* after knowledge, and *liftest up* thy voice
for understanding; if thou seekest her as silver, and
searchest for her as *for hid* treasures; *then* shalt thou
understand the fear of the Lord, and find the knowledge
of God [1]."

This is a subject which cannot too strongly be insisted
on. Act up to your light, though in the midst of
difficulties, and you will be carried on, you do not
know how far. Abraham obeyed the call and journeyed,
not knowing whither he went; so we, if we follow the
voice of God, shall be brought on step by step into a
new world, of which before we had no idea. This is
His gracious way with us: He gives, not all at once,
but by measure and season, wisely. To him that hath,
more shall be given. But we must begin at the begin-

[1] Prov. ii. 3—5.

ning. Each truth has its own order; we cannot join the way of life at any point of the course we please; we cannot learn advanced truths before we have learned primary ones. "Call upon Me," says the Divine Word, "and I will answer thee, and show thee great and mighty things which thou knowest not [1]." Religious men are always learning; but when men refuse to profit by light already granted, their light is turned to darkness. Observe our Lord's conduct with the Pharisees. They asked Him on what authority He acted. He gave them no direct answer, but referred them to the mission of John the Baptist—"The baptism of John, whence was it? from heaven or from men [2]?" They refused to say. Then He said, "Neither tell I you by what authority I do these things." That is, they would not profit by the knowledge they already had from St. John the Baptist, who spoke of Christ— therefore no more was given them.

All of us may learn a lesson here, for all of us are in danger of hastily finding fault with others, and condemning their opinions or practices; not considering, that unless we have faithfully obeyed our conscience and improved our talents, we are no fit judges of them at all. Christ and His Saints are alike destitute of form or comeliness in the eyes of the world, and it is only as we labour to change our nature, through God's help, and to serve Him truly, that we begin to discern the

[1] Jer. xxxiii. 3.   [2] Matt. xxi. 25.

beauty of holiness. Then, at length, we find reason to suspect our own judgments of what is truly good, and perceive our own blindness; for by degrees we find that those whose opinions and conduct we hitherto despised or wondered at as extravagant or unaccountable or weak, really know more than ourselves, and are above us—and so, ever as we rise in knowledge and grow in spiritual illumination, they (to our amazement) rise also, while we look at them. The better we are, the more we understand their excellence; till at length we are taught something of their Divine Master's perfections also, which before were hid from us, and see why it is that, though the Gospel is set on a hill in the midst of the world, like a city which cannot be hid, yet to multitudes it is notwithstanding hid, since He taketh the wise in their own craftiness, and the pure in heart alone can see God.

How are the sheep of Christ's flock scattered abroad in the waste world! He came to gather them together in one; but they wander again and faint by the way, as having lost their Shepherd. What religious opinion can be named which some men or other have not at some time held? All are equally confident in the truth of their own doctrines, though the many must be mistaken. In this confusion let us, my brethren, look to ourselves, each to himself. There must be a right and a wrong, and no matter whether others agree with us or not, it is to us a solemn practical concern not to turn away our ears from the truth. Let not the diversity of opinion in the world dismay you, or deter you from seeking all your life long true wisdom. It is not a search for this day or that, but as you should ever grow in grace, so should you ever grow also in the knowledge of our Lord and Saviour Jesus Christ. Care not for the perplexing question which many will put to you, " How can you be sure that you are right more than others ? " Others are nothing to you, if they are not holy and devout in their conversation—and we all know what is meant by being holy; we know whom we should call holy; to be holy is to be like an Apostle. Seek truth in the way of *obedience ;* try to act up to your conscience, and let your opinions be the result, not of mere chance reasoning or fancy, but of an improved heart. This way, I say, carries with it an evidence to ourselves of its being the right way, if any way be right; and that there is a right and a wrong way conscience also tells us. God surely will listen to none but those who strive to obey Him. Those who thus proceed, watching, praying, taking all means given them of gaining the truth, studying the Scriptures, and doing their duty; in short, those who seek religious truth by principle and habit, as the main business of their lives, humbly not arrogantly, peaceably not contentiously, shall not be " turned unto fables." " The secret of the Lord is with them that fear Him ;" but in proportion as we are conscious to ourselves that we are indolent, and transgress

our own sense of right and wrong, in the same proportion we have cause to fear, not only that we are not in a
safe state, but, further than this, that we do not know
what is a safe state, and what an unsafe—what is light
and what is darkness, what is truth and what is error;
which way leads to heaven and which to hell. "The
way of the wicked is in darkness; they know not at
what they stumble [1]."

I know we shall find it very hard to rouse ourselves,
to break the force of habit, to resolve to serve God, and
persevere in doing so. And assuredly we must expect,
even at best, and with all our efforts, perhaps back-
slidings, and certainly much continual imperfection all
through our lives, in all we do. But this should create
in us a horror of disobedience, not a despair at over-
coming ourselves. We are not under the law of nature,
but under grace; we are not bid do a thing above our
strength, because, though our hearts are naturally weak,
we are not left to ourselves. According to the command, so is the gift. God's grace is sufficient for us.
Why, then, should we fear? Rather, why should we not
make any sacrifice, and give up all that is naturally
pleasing to us, rather than that light and truth should
have come into the world, yet we not find them? Let
us be willing to endure toil and trouble; and should
times of comparative quiet be given to us, should for a
while temptation be withdrawn, or the Spirit of comfort

[1] Prov. iv. 19.

poured upon us, let us not inconsiderately rest in these accidental blessings. While we thank God for them, let us remember that in its turn the time of labour and fear, and danger and anxiety, will come upon us; and that we must act our part well in it. We live here to struggle and to endure: the time of eternal rest will come hereafter.

"Blessed are the undefiled in the way, who walk in the law of the Lord. Blessed are they that keep His testimonies, and that seek Him with the whole heart[1]." "The path of the just is as the shining light, that shineth more and more unto the perfect day[2]."

[1] Ps. cxix. 1, 2.   [2] Prov. iv. 18.

SERMON XIV.

Obedience to God the Way to Faith in Christ.

"When Jesus saw that he answered discreetly, He said unto him, Thou art not far from the kingdom of God."—MARK xii. 34.

THE answer of the scribe, which our blessed Lord here commends, was occasioned by Christ's setting before him the two great commandments of the Law. When He had declared the love of God and of man to comprehend our whole duty, the scribe said, "Master, Thou hast said the truth: for there is one God; and there is none other but He: and to love Him with all the heart, and with all the understanding, and with all the soul, and with all the strength, and to love his neighbour as himself, is more than all whole burnt-offerings and sacrifices." Upon this acknowledgment of the duty of general religious obedience, Christ replied, in the words of the text, "Thou art not far from the kingdom of God," i. e. Thou art not far from being a Christian.

In these words, then, we are taught, first, that the

Christian's faith and obedience are not the same religion as that of natural conscience, as being some way beyond it; secondly, that this way is "not far," not far in the case of those who try to act up to their conscience; in other words, that obedience to conscience leads to obedience to the Gospel, which, instead of being something different altogether, is but the completion and perfection of that religion which natural conscience teaches.

Indeed, it would have been strange if the God of nature had said one thing, and the God of grace another; if the truths which our conscience taught us without the information of Scripture, were contradicted by that information when obtained. But it is not so; there are not two ways of pleasing God; what conscience suggests, Christ has sanctioned and explained; to love God and our neighbour are the great duties of the Gospel as well as of the Law; he who endeavours to fulfil them by the light of nature is in the way towards, is, as our Lord said, "not far from Christ's kingdom;" for to him that hath more shall be given.

It is not in one or two places merely that this same doctrine is declared to us; indeed, all revelation is grounded on those simple truths which our own consciences teach us in a measure, though a poor measure, even without it. It is One God, and none other but He, who speaks first in our consciences, then in His Holy Word; and, lest we should be in any difficulty about the matter, He has most mercifully told us so in

Scripture, wherein He refers again and again (as in the passage connected with the text) to the great Moral Law, as the foundation of the truth, which His Apostles and Prophets, and last of all His Son, have taught us: "Fear God, and keep His commandments; for this is the whole duty of man[1]."

Yet though this is so plain, both from our own moral sense, and the declarations of Scripture, still for many reasons it is necessary to insist upon it; chiefly, because, it being very hard to keep God's commandments, men would willingly persuade themselves, if they could, that strict obedience is not necessary under the Gospel, and that something else will be taken, for Christ's sake, in the stead of it. Instead of labouring, under God's grace, to change their wills, to purify their hearts, and so prepare themselves for the kingdom of God, they imagine that in that kingdom they may be saved by something short of this, by their baptism, or by their ceremonial observances (the burnt offerings and sacrifices which the scribe disparages), or by their correct knowledge of the truth, or by their knowledge of their own sinfulness, or by some past act of faith which is to last them during their lives, or by some strong habitual persuasion that they are safe; or, again, by the performance of some one part of their duty, though they neglect the rest, as if God said a thing to us in nature, and Christ unsaid it; and, when men wish a thing, it is not hard to find

[1] Eccles. xii. 13.

texts in Scripture which may be ingeniously perverted to suit their purpose. The error then being so common in practice, of believing that Christ came to gain for us easier terms of admittance into heaven than we had before (whereas, in fact, instead of making obedience less strict, He has enabled us to obey God more strictly; and instead of gaining *easier* terms of *admittance*, He has gained us *altogether* our admittance into heaven, which before was closed against us); this error, I say, being so common, it may be right to insist on the opposite truth, however obvious, that obedience to God is the way to know and believe in Christ.

1. Now, first, let us consider how plainly we are taught in Scripture that perfect obedience is the standard of Gospel holiness. By St. Paul: " Be not conformed to this world: but be ye transformed by the renewing of your mind, that ye may prove what is that good, and acceptable, and perfect, will of God [1]." " Circumcision is nothing, and uncircumcision is nothing, but the keeping of the commandments of God [2]." "Whatsoever things are true . . honest . . just . . pure . . lovely . . of good report: if there be any virtue, and if there be any praise, think on these things [3]." By St. James: " Whosoever shall keep the whole law, and yet offend in one point, he is guilty of all [4]." By St. Peter: " Giving all diligence, add to

---

[1] Rom. xii. 2.
[3] Phil. iv. 8.

[2] 1 Cor. vii. 19.
[4] James ii. 10.

your faith virtue . . knowledge . . temperance . patience . . godliness . . brotherly kindness . . charity [1]." By St. John: "Hereby do we know that we know Him, if we keep His commandments." Lastly, by our Lord Himself: "He that hath My commandments, and keepeth them, he it is that loveth Me: and he that loveth Me, shall be loved of My Father, and I will love him, and will manifest Myself to him [2]." And, above all, the following clear declaration in the Sermon on the Mount: "Whosoever . . shall break one of these least commandments, and shall teach men so, he shall be called the least in the kingdom of heaven: but whosoever shall do and teach them, the same shall be called great in the kingdom of heaven [3]."

These texts, and a multitude of others, show that the Gospel leaves us just where it found us, as regards the necessity of our obedience to God; that Christ has not obeyed instead of us, but that obedience is quite as imperative as if Christ had never come; nay, is pressed upon us with additional sanctions; the difference being, not that He relaxes the strict rule of keeping His commandments, but that He gives us spiritual aids, which we have not except through Him, to enable us to keep them. Accordingly Christ's service is represented in Scripture, not as different from that religious obedience which conscience teaches us naturally, but as the perfection of it, as I have already said. We are told again

[1] 2 Pet. i. 5—7. [2] John xiv. 21. [3] Matt. v. 19.

and again, that obedience to God leads on to faith in
Christ; that it is the only recognized way to Christ;
and that, therefore, to believe in Him, ordinarily implies
that we are living in obedience to God.   For instance :
" Every man . . . that hath heard and hath learned of
the Father, cometh unto Me [1];" " He that doeth truth,
cometh to the light [2]," i. e. to Christ; " No man can
come to Me, except the Father which hath sent Me,
draw him;" " If any man will do the will of God, he
shall know of the doctrine [3]."   On the other hand :
" He that hateth Me, hateth My Father also [4];" " If
ye had known Me, ye should have known My Father
also [5];" " Whosoever denieth the Son, the same hath
not the Father [6];" " Whosoever transgresseth, and
abideth not in the doctrine of Christ, hath not God : he
that abideth in the doctrine of Christ, he hath both the
Father and the Son [7]."

In these and other passages of Scripture we learn,
that though Christ came to be the light of the world,
yet He is not and cannot be a light to all, but to those
only who seek Him in the way of His commandments;
and to all others He is hid, the god of this world
" blinding the minds of them which believe not, lest the
light of the glorious Gospel of Christ, who is the Image
of God, should shine unto them [8]."

---

[1] John vi. 45.   [2] John iii. 21.   [3] John vii. 17.
[4] John xv. 23.   [5] John viii. 19.   [6] 1 John ii 23.
              [7] 2 John 9.   [8] 2 Cor. iv. 4.

2. And if we look to the history of the first propaga-
tion of the Gospel, we find this view confirmed. As far
as we can trace the history, we find the early Christian
Church was principally composed of those who had long
been in the habit of obeying their consciences carefully,
and so preparing themselves for Christ's religion, that
kingdom of God from which the text says they were not
far. Zacharias and Elisabeth, to whom the approach of
Christ's kingdom was first revealed, are described as
"both righteous before God, walking in all the commandments and ordinances of the Lord, blameless[1]."
Joseph, St. Mary's husband, is called "a just man[2];"
Simeon is spoken of as "a just and devout[3]" man;
Nathaniel, as "an Israelite in whom was no guile[4];"
Joseph of Arimathea was "a good man and a just[5];"
Cornelius, the centurion, was a "religious man, and one
that feared God with all his house, who gave much
alms to the people, and prayed to God alway[6]." And
in the book of Acts generally, we shall find (as far as
we are told any thing) that those chiefly were addressed
and converted by St. Paul, who had previously trained
themselves in a religious life:—At Perga, St. Paul
addressed the Israelites and those who feared God, not
the mere thoughtless heathen; and many of these followed him[7]. At Thessalonica a great multitude of

[1] Luke i. 6.   [2] Matt. i. 19.   [3] Luke ii. 25.
[4] John i. 47.   [5] Luke xxiii. 50.   [6] Acts x. 2.
[7] Acts xiii.

religious Greeks believed[1]; and at Athens the Apostle still disputed with the Jews, and with the professedly religious persons, though he also addressed the educated heathens who lived there. Here then is much evidence that Christ and His Apostles chiefly sought and found their first followers, not among open sinners, but among those who were endeavouring, however imperfectly, to obey God.

But it may be asked, Did Christ hold out no hope for those who had lived in sin? Doubtless He did, if they determined to forsake their sin. He came to save all, whatever their former life, who gave themselves up to Him as their Lord and Saviour; and in His Church He gathered together of every kind, those who had departed from God, as well as those who had ever served Him well. Open sinners must have a beginning of repentance, if they are to repent; and on this first beginning Christ invites them to Him at once, without delay, for pardon and for aid. But this is not the question; of course all who come to Him will be received; none will be cast out[2]. But the question is, not this, but whether they are likely to come, to hear His voice, and to follow Him; again, whether they will, generally speaking, prove as consistent and deeply-taught Christians as those who, compared with them, have never departed from God at all; and here all the advantage, doubtless, is on the side of those who (in the

---

[1] Acts xvii.　　　　　　　　　[2] John iv. 3. 7.

words of Scripture) have walked in the ordinances of
the Lord blameless [1]. When sinners truly repent, then,
indeed, they are altogether brothers in Christ's kingdom
with those who have not in the same sense "need of
repentance;" but that they should repent at all is
(alas!) so far from being likely, that when the unexpected event takes place it causes such joy in heaven
(from the marvellousness of it) as is not even excited by
the ninety and nine just persons who need no such
change of mind [2]. Of such changes some instances are
given us in the Gospels for the encouragement of all
penitents, such as that of the woman, mentioned by
St. Luke, who "loved much." Christ most graciously
went among sinners, if so be He might save them; and
we know that even those open sinners, when they knew
that they were sinners, were nearer salvation, and in a
better state, than the covetous and irreligious Pharisees,
who added to their other gross sins, hypocrisy, blindness, a contempt of others, and a haughty and superstitious reliance on the availing virtue of their religious
privileges.

And, moreover, of these penitents of whom I speak—
and whom, when they become penitents, we cannot love
too dearly (after our Saviour's pattern), nay, or reverence
too highly, and whom the Apostles, after Christ's
departure, brought into the Church in such vast multitudes—none, as far as we know, had any sudden change

[1] Luke i. 6.   [2] Luke xv. 7.

of mind from bad to good wrought in them; nor do we hear of any of them honoured with any important station in the Church. Great as St. Paul's sin was in persecuting Christ's followers, before his conversion, that sin was of a different kind; he was not transgressing, but obeying his conscience (however blinded it was); he was doing what he thought his duty, when he was arrested by the heavenly vision, which, when presented to him, he at once " obeyed;" he was not sinning *against light*, but *in* darkness. We know nothing of the precise state of his mind immediately before his conversion; but we do know thus much, that years elapsed after his conversion before he was employed as an Apostle in the Church of God.

I have confined myself to the time of Christ's coming; but not only then, but at all times and under all circumstances, as all parts of the Bible inform us, obedience to the light we possess is the way to gain more light. In the words of Wisdom, in the book of Proverbs, " I love them that love Me; and those that seek Me early shall find Me. . . . I lead in the way of righteousness, in the midst of the paths of judgment [1]." Or, in the still more authoritative words of Christ Himself, " He that is faithful in that which is least, is faithful also in much [2];" and, " He that hath, to him shall be given [3]."

[1] Prov. viii. 17. 20. [2] Luke xvi. 10.

[3] Mark iv. 25.

Now let us see some of the consequences which follow from this great Scripture truth.

1. First of all, we see the hopelessness of waiting for any sudden change of heart, if we are at present living in sin. Far more persons deceive themselves by some such vain expectation than at first sight may appear. That there are even many irreligious men, who, from hearing the false doctrines now so common, and receiving general impressions from them, look forward for a possible day when God will change their hearts by His own mere power, in spite of themselves, and who thus get rid of the troublesome thought that now they are in a state of fearful peril; who say they can do nothing till His time comes, while still they acknowledge themselves to be far from Him; even this I believe to be a fact, strange and gross as the self-deception may appear to be. And others, too, many more, doubtless, are there who, not thinking themselves far from Him, but, on the contrary, high in His favour, still, by a dreadful deceit of Satan, are led to be indolent and languid in their obedience to His commandments, from a pretence that they can do nothing of themselves, and must wait for the successive motions of God's grace to excite them to action. The utmost these persons do is to talk of religion, when they ought to be up and active, and waiting for the Blessed Spirit of Christ by obeying God's will. "Awake thou that sleepest, and arise from the dead, and Christ shall give thee

light[1]." This is the exhortation. And doubtless to all those who live a self-indulgent life, however they veil their self-indulgence from themselves by a notion of their superior religious knowledge, and by their faculty of speaking fluently in Scripture language, to all such the word of life says, "Be not deceived; God is not mocked;" He tries the heart, and disdains the mere worship of the lips. He acknowledges no man as a believer in His Son, who does not anxiously struggle to obey His commandments to the utmost; to none of those who seek without striving, and who consider themselves safe, to none of these does He give "power to become sons of God[2]." Be not deceived; such have fallen from that state in which their baptism placed them and are "far from the kingdom of God." "Whatsoever a man soweth, that shall he also reap[3]." And if any one says that St. Paul was converted suddenly, and without his exerting himself, it is sufficient to reply, that, guilty as St. Paul was, his guilt was not that of indolence, and self-indulgence, and indifference. His sin was that of *neglecting the study of Scripture;* and thus, missing the great truth that Jesus was the Christ, he persecuted the Christians; but though his conscience was ill-informed, and that by his own fault, yet he obeyed it such as it was. He did what he did ignorantly. If then the case really be that St. Paul *was* suddenly converted, hence, it is true, some kind of

---

[1] Eph. v. 14. [2] John i. 12. [3] Gal. vi. 7

vague hope may be said to be held out to furious, intolerant bigots, and bloodthirsty persecutors, if they are acting in consequence of their own notions of duty; none to the slothful and negligent and lukewarm; none *but* to those who can say, with St. Paul, that they have "lived in all good conscience before God until this day [1];" and that not under an easy profession, but in a straitest religious sect, giving themselves up to their duty, and following the law of God, though in ignorance, yet with all their heart and soul.

2. But, after all, there are very many more than I have as yet mentioned, who wait for a time of repentance to come while at present they live in sin. For instance, the young, who consider it will be time enough to think of God when they grow old; that religion will then come as a matter of course, and that they will then like it naturally, just as they now like their follies and sins. Or those who are much engaged in worldly business, who confess they do not give that attention to religion which they ought to give; who neglect the ordinances of the Church; who desecrate the Lord's day; who give little or no time to the study of God's word; who allow themselves in various small transgressions of their conscience, and resolutely harden themselves against the remorse which such transgressions are calculated to cause them; and all this they do under the idea that at length a convenient season will come

[1] Acts xxiii. 1.

when they may give themselves to religious duties. They determine on retiring at length from the world, and of making up for lost time by greater diligence then. All such persons, and how many they are! think that they will be able to seek Christ when they please, though they have lived all their lives with no true love either of God or man; i. e. they do not, in their hearts, believe our Lord's doctrine contained in the text, that to obey God is to be near Christ, and that to disobey is to be far from Him.

How will this truth be plain to us in that day when the secrets of all hearts shall be revealed! *Now* we do not believe that strict obedience is as necessary as it is. I say we do *not* believe it, though we say we do. No one, of course, believes it in its fulness, but most of us are deceived by words, and say we accept and believe, when we hardly do more than profess it. We say, indeed, that obedience is absolutely necessary, and are surprised to have our real belief in what we say questioned; but we do not give the truth that place in the scheme of our religion which this profession requires, and thus we cheat our consciences. We put something *before* it, in our doctrinal system, as *more* necessary than it; one man puts faith, another outward devotion, a third attention to his temporal calling, another zeal for the Church; that is, we put a part for the whole of our duty, and so run the risk of losing our souls. These are the burnt-offerings and sacrifices which even the scribe put aside before the weightier matters of the Law. Or again, we fancy that the means of gaining heaven are something stranger and rarer than the mere obvious duty of obedience to God; we are loth to seek Christ in the waters of Jordan rather than in Pharpar and Abana, rivers of Damascus; we prefer to seek Him in the height above, or to descend into the deep, rather than to believe that the word is nigh us, even in our mouth and in our heart [1]. Hence, in false religions some men have even tortured themselves and been cruel to their flesh, thereby to become as gods, and to mount aloft; and in our own, with a not less melancholy, though less self-denying, error, men fancy that certain strange effects on their minds—strong emotion, restlessness, and an unmanly excitement and extravagance of thought and feeling—are the tokens of that inscrutable Spirit, who is given us, not to make us something *other than* men, but to make us, what without His gracious aid we never shall be, upright, self-mastering men, humble and obedient children of our Lord and Saviour.

In that day of trial all these deceits will be laid aside; we shall stand in our own real form, whether it be of heaven or of earth, the wedding garment, or the old raiment of sin [2]; and then, how many (do we think) will be revealed as the heirs of light, who have followed Christ in His narrow way, and humbled themselves after His manner (though not in His perfection, and with

[1] Rom. x. 8.   [2] Zech. iii. 4.

nothing of His merit) to the daily duties of soberness, mercy, gentleness, self-denial, and the fear of God?

These, be they many or few, will then receive their prize from Him who died for them, who has made them what they are, and completes in heaven what first by conscience, then by His Spirit, He began here. Surely they were despised on the earth by the world; both by the open sinners, who thought their scrupulousness to be foolishness, and by such pretenders to God's favour as thought it ignorance. But, in reality, they had received from their Lord the treasures both of wisdom and of knowledge, though men knew it not; and they then will be acknowledged by Him before all creatures, as heirs of the glory prepared for them before the beginning of the world.

SERMON XV.

Sudden Conversions.

" By the grace of God I am what I am : and His grace which was bestowed upon me was not in vain."—I COR. xv. 10.

WE can hardly conceive that grace, such as that given to the great Apostle who speaks in the text, would have been given in vain; that is, we should not expect that it would have been given, had it been foreseen and designed by the Almighty Giver that it would have been in vain. By which I do not mean, of course, to deny that God's gifts are oftentimes abused and wasted by man, which they are; but, when we consider the wonderful mode of St. Paul's conversion, and the singular privilege granted him, the only one of men of whom is clearly recorded the privilege of seeing Christ with his bodily eyes after His ascension, as is alluded to shortly before the text; I say, considering these high and extraordinary favours vouchsafed to the Apostle, we should naturally suppose that some great objects in the history of the Church were contemplated

by means of them, such as in the event were fulfilled.
We cannot tell, indeed, why God works, or by what
rule He chooses; we must always be sober and humble
in our thoughts about His ways, which are infinitely
above our ways; but what would be speculation, perhaps venturous speculation, before the event, at least
becomes a profitable meditation after it. At least, now,
when we read and dwell on St. Paul's history, we may
discern and insist upon the suitableness of his character,
before his conversion, for that display of free grace
which was made in him. Not that he could merit such
a great mercy—the idea is absurd as well as wicked;
but that such a one as he was before God's grace,
naturally grew by the aid of it into what he was afterwards as a Christian.

His, indeed, was a "wonderful conversion," as our
Church in one place calls it, because it was so unexpected, and (as far as the appearance went) so sudden.
Who of the suffering Christians, against whom he was
raging so furiously, could have conceived that their
enemy was to be the great preacher and champion of
the despised Cross? Does God work miracles to reclaim His open malevolent adversaries, and not rather
to encourage and lead forward those who timidly seek
Him?

It may be useful, then, to mention one or two kinds
of what may be called sudden conversions, to give
some opinion on the character of each of them, and to

inquire which of them really took place in St. Paul's case.

1. First; some men turn to religion all at once from some sudden impulse of mind, some powerful excitement, or some strong persuasion. It is a sudden resolve that comes upon them. Now such cases occur very frequently where religion has nothing to do with the matter, and then we think little about it, merely calling the persons who thus change all at once volatile and light-minded. Thus there are persons who all of a sudden give up some pursuit which they have been eagerly set upon, or change from one trade or calling to another, or change their opinions as regards the world's affairs. Every one knows the impression left upon the mind by such instances. The persons thus changing may be, and often are, amiable, kind, and pleasant, as companions; but we cannot depend on them; and we pity them, as believing they are doing harm both to their temporal interests and to their own minds. Others there are who almost profess to love change for change-sake; they think the pleasure of life consists in seeing first one thing, then another; variety is their chief good; and it is a sufficient objection in their minds to any pursuit or recreation, that it is old. These, too, pass suddenly and capriciously from one subject to another. So far in matters of daily life;—but when such a person exhibits a similar changeableness in his religious views, then men begin to be astonished, and look out with

curiosity or anxiety to see what is the meaning of it; and particularly if the individual who thus suddenly changed, was very decided before in the particular course of life which he then followed. For instance, supposing he not merely professed no deep religious impressions, but actually was unbelieving or profligate; or, again, supposing he not merely professed himself of this creed or that, but was very warm, and even bitter in the enforcement of it; then, I say, men wonder, though they do not wonder at similar infirmities in matters of this world.

Nor can I say that they are wrong in being alive to such changes; we *ought* to feel differently with reference to religious subjects, and not be as unconcerned about them as we are about the events of time. Did a man suddenly inform us, with great appearance of earnestness, that he had seen an accident in the street, or did he say that he had seen a miracle, I confess it is natural, nay, in the case of most men, certainly in the case of the uneducated, far more religious, to feel differently towards these two accounts; to feel shocked, indeed, but not awed, at the first—to feel a certain solemn astonishment and pious reverence at the news of the miracle. For a religious mind is ever looking towards God, and seeking His traces; referring all events to Him, and desirous of His explanation of them; and when to such a one information is brought that God has in some extraordinary way showed Himself, he *will* at first sight be tempted to believe it, and it is only the experience of the number of deceits and false prophecies which are in the world, his confidence in the Catholic Church which he sees before him, and which is his guide into the truth, and (if he be educated) his enlightened views concerning the course and laws of God's providence, which keep him steady and make him hard to believe such stories. On the other hand, men destitute of religion altogether, of course from the first ridicule such accounts, and, as the event shows, rightly; and yet, in spite of this, they are not so worthy our regard as those who at first were credulous, from having some religious principle without enough religious knowledge. Therefore, I am not surprised that such sudden conversions as I have been describing deceive for a time even the better sort of people—whom I should blame, if I were called on to do so, not so much for the mere fact of their believing readily, but for their not believing the Church; for believing private individuals who have no authority more than the Church, and for not recollecting St. Paul's words, "If any man . . . though we, or an Angel from heaven, preach any other Gospel unto you than that ye have received, let him be accursed[1]."

2. In the cases of sudden conversion I have been speaking of, when men change at once either from open sin, or again from the zealous partizanship of a certain creed, to some novel form of faith or worship, their light-

[1] Gal. i. 8, 9.

mindedness is detected by their frequent changing—their changing again and again, so that one can never be certain of them. This is the test of their unsoundness; —having no root in themselves, their convictions and earnestness quickly wither away. But there is another kind of sudden conversion, which I proceed to mention, in which a man perseveres to the end, consistent in the new form he adopts, and which may be right or wrong, as it happens, but which *he* cannot be said to recommend or confirm to us by his own change. I mean when a man, for some reason or other, whether in religion or not, takes a great disgust to his present course of life, and suddenly abandons it for another. This is the case of those who rush from one to the other extreme, and it generally arises from strong and painful feeling, unsettling and, as it were, revolutionizing the mind. A story is told of a spendthrift who, having ruined himself by his extravagances, went out of doors to meditate on his own folly and misery, and in the course of a few hours returned home a determined miser, and was for the rest of his life remarkable for covetousness and penuriousness. This is not more extraordinary than the fickleness of mind just now described. In like manner, men sometimes will change suddenly from love to hatred, from over-daring to cowardice. These are no amiable changes, whether arising or not from bodily malady, as is sometimes the case; nor do they impart any credit or sanction to the particular secular course or habit of mind adopted on the change : neither do they in religion therefore. A man who suddenly professes religion after a profligate life, merely because he is sick of his vices, or tormented by the thought of God's anger, which is the consequence of them, and without the love of God, does no honour to religion, for he might, if it so chanced, turn a miser or a misanthrope; and, therefore, though religion is not at all the less holy and true because he submits himself to it, and though doubtless it is a much better thing for *him* that he turns to religion than that he should become a miser or a misanthrope, still, when he acts on such motives as I have described, he cannot be said to do any honour to the cause of religion by his conversion. Yet it is such persons who at various times have been thought great saints, and been reckoned to recommend and prove the truth of the Gospel to the world !

Now if any one asks what test there is that this kind of sudden conversion is not from God, as instability and frequent change are the test, on the other hand, in disproof of the divinity of the conversions just now mentioned, I answer,—its moroseness, inhumanity, and unfitness for this world. Men who change through strong passion and anguish become as hard and as rigid as stone or iron; they are not fit for life; they are only fit for the solitudes in which they sometimes bury themselves; they can only do one or two of their duties, and that only in one way; they do not indeed change their principles, as the fickle convert, but, on the other hand, they cannot apply, adapt, accommodate, modify, diversify their principles to the existing state of things, which is the opposite fault. They do not aim at a perfect obedience in little things as well as great; and a most serious fault it is, looking at it merely as a matter of practice, and without any reference to the views and motives from which it proceeds; most opposed is it to the spirit of true religion, which is intended to fit us for all circumstances of life as they come, in order that we may be humble, docile, ready, patient, and cheerful,—in order that we may really show ourselves God's servants, who do all things for Him, coming when He calleth, going when He sendeth, doing this or that at His bidding. So much for the practice of such men; and when we go higher, and ask *why* they are thus formal and unbending in their mode of life, what are the principles that make them thus harsh and unserviceable, I fear we must trace it to some form of selfishness and pride; the same principles which, under other circumstances, would change the profligate into the covetous and parsimonious.

I think it will appear at once that St. Paul's conversion, however it was effected, and whatever was the process of it, resembled neither the one nor the other of these. That it was not the change of a fickle mind is shown by his firmness in keeping to his new faith— by his constancy unto death, a death of martyrdom.

That it was not the change of a proud and disappointed mind, quitting with disgust what he once loved too well, is evidenced by the variety of his labours, his active services, and continued presence in the busy thoroughfares of the world; by the cheerfulness, alacrity, energy, dexterity, and perseverance, with which he pleaded the cause of God among sinners. He reminds us of his firmness, as well as gentleness, when he declares, "What mean ye to weep, and break my heart? for I am ready not to be bound only, but also to die at Jerusalem for the Name of the Lord Jesus;" and of his ready accommodation of himself to the will of God, in all its forms, when he says, "I am made all things to all men, that I might by all means save some [1]."

3. But there is another kind of sudden conversion, or rather what appears to be such, not uncommonly found, and which may be that to which St. Paul's conversion is to be referred, and which I proceed to describe.

When men change their religious opinions really and truly, it is not merely their opinions that they change, but their hearts; and this evidently is not done in a moment—it is a slow work; nevertheless, though gradual, the change is often not uniform, but proceeds, so to say, by fits and starts, being influenced by external events, and other circumstances. This we see in the growth of plants, for instance; it is slow, gradual, continual; yet one day by chance they grow more than another, they

[1] Acts xxi. 13. 1 Cor. ix. 22.

make a shoot, or at least we are attracted to their growth on that day by some accidental circumstance, and it remains on our memory. So with our souls: we all, by nature, are far from God; nay, and we have all characters to form, which is a work of time. All this must have a beginning; and those who are now leading religious lives have begun at different times. Baptism, indeed, is God's time, when He first gives us grace; but alas! through the perverseness of our will, we do not follow Him. There must be a time then for beginning. Many men do not at all recollect any one marked and definite time *when* they began to seek God. Others recollect a time, not, properly speaking, when they began, but when they made what may be called a shoot forward, the fact either being so, in consequence of external events, or at least for some reason or other their attention being called to it. Others, again, continue forming a religious character and religious opinions as the result of it, though holding at the same time some outward profession of faith inconsistent with them; as, for instance, suppose it has been their unhappy condition to be brought up as heathens, Jews, infidels, or heretics. They hold the notions they have been taught for a long while, not perceiving that the character forming within them is at variance with these, till at length the inward growth forces itself forward, forces on the opinions accompanying it, and the dead outward surface of error, which has no root in their minds, from some accidental occurrence, suddenly falls off; suddenly, —just as a building might suddenly fall, which had been going many years, and which falls at this moment rather than that, in consequence of some chance cause, as it is called, which we cannot detect.

Now in all these cases one point of time is often taken by religious men, as if the very time of conversion, and as if it were sudden, though really, as is plain, in none of them is there any suddenness in the matter. In the last of these instances, which might be in a measure, if we dare say it, St. Paul's case, the time when the formal outward profession of error fell off, is taken as the time of conversion. Others recollect the first occasion when any deep serious thought came into their minds, and reckon this as the date of their inward change. Others, again, recollect some intermediate point of time when they first openly professed their faith, or dared do some noble deed for Christ's sake.

I might go on to show more particularly how what I have said applies to St. Paul; but as this would take too much time I will only observe generally, that there was much in St. Paul's character which was not changed on his conversion, but merely directed to other and higher objects, and purified; it was his creed that was changed, and his soul by regeneration; and though he was sinning most grievously and awfully when Christ appeared to him from heaven, he evidenced then, as afterwards, a most burning energetic zeal for God, a most scrupulous strictness of life, an abstinence from all self-indulgence, much more from all approach to sensuality or sloth, and an implicit obedience to what he considered God's will. It was pride which was his inward enemy—pride which needed an overthrow. He acted rather as a defender and protector, than a minister of what he considered the truth; he relied on his own views; he was positive and obstinate; he did not seek for light as a little child; he did not look out for a Saviour who was to come, and he missed Him when He came.

But how great was the change in these respects when he became a servant of Him whom he had persecuted! As he had been conspicuous for a proud confidence in self, on his privileges, on his knowledge, on his birth, on his observances, so he became conspicuous for his humility. What self-abasement, when he says, "I am the least of the Apostles, that am not meet to be called an Apostle, because I persecuted the Church of God; but by the grace of God I am what I am." What keen and bitter remembrance of the past, when he says, "Who was before a blasphemer, and a persecutor, and injurious; but I obtained mercy, because I did it ignorantly in unbelief[1]." Ah! what utter self-abandonment, what scorn and hatred of self, when he, who had been so pleased to be a Hebrew of Hebrews, and a Pharisee, bore to be called, nay gloried for Christ's sake in being

[1] 1 Tim. i. 13.

called, an apostate, the most odious and miserable of titles!—bore to be spurned and spit upon as a renegade, a traitor, a false-hearted and perfidious, a fallen, a lost son of his Church; a shame to his mother, and a curse to his countrymen. · Such was the light in which those furious zealots looked on the great Apostle, who bound themselves together by an oath that they would neither eat nor drink till they had killed him. It was their justification in their own eyes, that he was a "pestilent fellow," a "stirrer of seditions," and an abomination amid sacred institutions which God had given.

And, lastly, what supported him in this great trial? that special mercy which converted him, which he, and he only, saw—the Face of Jesus Christ. That all-pitying, all-holy eye, which turned in love upon St. Peter when he denied Him, and thereby roused him to repentance, looked on St. Paul also, while he persecuted Him, and wrought in him a sudden conversion. "Last of all," he says, "He was seen of me also, as of one born out of due time." One sight of that Divine Countenance, so tender, so loving, so majestic, so calm, was enough, first to convert him, then to support him on his way amid the bitter hatred and fury which he was to excite in those who hitherto had loved him.

And if such be the effect of a momentary vision of the glorious Presence of Christ, what think you, my brethren, will be their bliss, to whom it shall be given, this life ended, to see that Face eternally?

SERMON XVI.

The Shepherd of our Souls.

" I am the good Shepherd: the good Shepherd giveth His life for the sheep."
—JOHN x. 11.

OUR Lord here appropriates to Himself the title under which He had been foretold by the Prophets. "David My servant shall be king over them," says Almighty God by the mouth of Ezekiel: "and they all shall have one Shepherd." And in the book of Zechariah, " Awake, O sword, against My Shepherd, and against the man that is My fellow, saith the Lord of Hosts; smite the Shepherd, and the sheep shall be scattered." And in like manner St. Peter speaks of our returning "to the Shepherd and Bishop of our souls [1]."

"The good Shepherd giveth His life for the sheep." In those countries of the East where our Lord appeared, the office of a shepherd is not only a lowly and simple office, and an office of trust, as it is with us, but, moreover, an office of great hardship and of peril. Our flocks

---

[1] Ezek. xxxvii. 24. Zech. xiii. 7. 1 Pet. ii. 25.

are exposed to no enemies, such as our Lord describes.
The Shepherd here has no need to prove his fidelity to
the sheep by encounters with fierce beasts of prey. The
hireling shepherd is not tried. But where our Lord
dwelt in the days of His flesh it was otherwise. There
it was true that the good Shepherd giveth His life for
the sheep—"but he that is an hireling, and whose own
the sheep are not, seeth the wolf coming, and leaveth
the sheep, and fleeth, and the wolf catcheth them and
scattereth the sheep. The hireling fleeth, because he is
an hireling, and careth not for the sheep."

Our Lord found the sheep scattered; or, as He had said
shortly before, "All that ever came before Me are thieves
and robbers;" and in consequence the sheep had no guide.
Such were the priests and rulers of the Jews when Christ
came; so that "when He saw the multitudes He was
moved with compassion on them, because they fainted,
and were scattered abroad as sheep having no shepherd [1]."
Such, in like manner, were the rulers and prophets of Israel
in the days of Ahab, when Micaiah, the Lord's Prophet,
"saw all Israel scattered on the hills, as sheep that have
not a shepherd, and the Lord said, These have no Master, let them return every man to his house in peace [2]."
Such, too, were the shepherds in the time of Ezekiel,
of whom the Prophet says, "Woe be to the shepherds
of Israel that do feed themselves! should not the shepherd feed the flocks? . . . . They were scattered, because

[1] Matt. ix. 36.   [2] 1 Kings xxii. 17.

there is no shepherd : and they became meat to all the
beasts of the field, when they were scattered [1] :" and in
the time of the Prophet Zechariah, who says, " Woe to
the idle shepherd that leaveth the flock [2] ! "

So was it all over the world when Christ came in His
infinite mercy " to gather in one the children of God that
were scattered abroad." And though for a moment,
when in the conflict with the enemy the good Shepherd
had to lay down His life for the sheep, they were left
without a guide (according to the prophecy already
quoted, " Smite the Shepherd and the sheep shall be
scattered "), yet He soon rose from death to live for
ever, according to that other prophecy which said, " He
that scattered Israel will gather him, as a shepherd doth
his flock [3]." And as He says Himself in the parable
before us, " He calleth His own sheep by name and
leadeth them out, and goeth before them, and the sheep
follow Him, for they know His voice," so, on His resurrection, while Mary wept, He did call her by her
name [4], and she turned herself and knew Him by the
ear whom she had not known by the eye. So, too, He
said, " Simon, son of Jonas, lovest thou Me [5]?" And
He added, " Follow Me." And so again He and His
Angel told the women, " Behold He goeth before you
into Galilee . . . go tell My brethren, that they go into
Galilee, and there shall they see Me."

---

[1] Ezek. xxxiv. 2. 5.   [2] Zech. xi. 17.   [3] Jer. xxxi. 10.
[4] John xx. 16.   [5] John xxi. 15.

From that time the good Shepherd who took the place of the sheep, and died that they might live for ever, has gone before them : and " they follow the Lamb whithersoever He goeth [1];" going their way forth by the footsteps of the flock, and feeding their kids beside the shepherds' tents [2].

No earthly images can come up to the awful and gracious truth, that God became the Son of man—that the Word became flesh, and was born of a woman. This ineffable mystery surpasses human words. No titles of earth can Christ give to Himself, ever so lowly or mean, which will fitly show us His condescension. His act and deed is too great even for His own lips to utter it. Yet He delights in the image contained in the text, as conveying to us, in such degree as we can receive it, some notion of the degradation, hardship, and pain, which He underwent for our sake.

Hence it was prophesied under this figure by the Prophet Isaiah, " Behold, the Lord God will come with strong hand, and His arm shall rule for Him . . . . He shall feed His flock like a shepherd : He shall gather the lambs with His arm, and carry them in His bosom, and shall gently lead those that are with young [3]." And, again, He promises by the mouth of Ezekiel, " Behold, I, even I, will both search My sheep, and seek them out. As a shepherd seeketh out his flock in the day that he is among his sheep that are scattered ; so

[1] Rev. xiv. 4.　　　[2] Cant. i. 8.　　　[3] Isa. xl. 10, 11.

will I seek out My sheep, and will deliver them out of
all places where they have been scattered in the cloudy
and dark day [1]." And the Psalmist says of Him, "The
Lord is my Shepherd, therefore can I lack nothing.
He shall feed me in a green pasture, and lead me forth
beside the waters of comfort [2]." And he addresses Him,
"Hear, O thou Shepherd of Israel, Thou that leadest
Joseph like a sheep, show Thyself also, Thou that sittest
upon the Cherubims [3]." And He Himself says in a
parable, speaking of Himself, "What man of you having
a hundred sheep, if he lose one of them, doth not leave
the ninety and nine in the wilderness, and go after that
which is lost, until he find it? And when he hath found
it, he layeth it on his shoulders, rejoicing [4]."

Observe, my brethren, it is here said that Christ, the
Lord of Angels, condescends to lay the lost sheep on
His shoulders: in a former passage of the Prophet
Isaiah it was said that He should "gather them with
His arm, and carry them in His bosom." By carrying
them in His bosom is meant the love He bears them,
and the fulness of His grace; by carrying them on His
shoulders is signified the security of their dwelling-place;
as of old time it was said of Benjamin, "the beloved of
the Lord shall dwell in safety by Him . . . and the
Lord shall cover him all the day long, and he shall
dwell between His shoulders [5];" and again, of Israel,

---

[1] Ezek. xxxiv. 11, 12.   [2] Ps. xxiii. 1, 2.   [3] Ps. lxxx. 1.
[4] Luke xv. 4, 5.   [5] Deut. xxxiii. 12.

"As an eagle stirreth up her nest, fluttereth over her young, spreadeth abroad her wings, taketh them, beareth them on her wings: so the Lord alone did lead him, and there was no strange god with him." And again, in the Prophet Isaiah, "Bel boweth down, Nebo stoopeth; their idols were upon the beasts and upon the cattle . . hearken unto Me, O house of Jacob . . which are carried *by Me* from the womb . . Even to your old age I am He, and even to hoary hairs will I carry you; I have made and I will bear, even I will carry, and will deliver you [1]." He alone, who "bowed Himself and came down," He alone could do it; He alone could bear a whole world's weight, the load of a guilty world, the burden of man's sin, the accumulated debt, past, present, and to come; the sufferings which we owed but could not pay, the wrath of God on the children of Adam; "in His own body on the tree [2]," "being made a curse for us [3]," "the just for the unjust, that He might bring us unto God," "through the Eternal Spirit offering Himself without spot to God, and purging our conscience from dead works to serve the Living God [4]." Such was the deed of Christ, laying down His life for us: and therefore He is called the Good Shepherd.

And hence, in like manner, from the time of Adam to that of Christ, a shepherd's work has been marked out with special Divine favour, as being a shadow of the

---

[1] Deut. xxxii. 11. Isa. xlvi. 1—4.   [2] 1 Pet. ii. 24.
[3] Gal. iii. 13.   [4] 1 Pet. iii. 18. Heb. ix. 14.

good Shepherd who was to come. "Righteous Abel" was "a keeper of sheep," "and in process of time" he "brought of the firstlings of his flock and of the fat thereof. And the Lord had respect unto Abel and to his offering[1]." And who were they to whom the Angels first brought the news that a Saviour was born? "Shepherds abiding in the field, keeping watch over their flock by night[2]." And what is the description given of the chosen family when they descended into Egypt? "Thy servants," they say, "are shepherds, both we and also our fathers[3];" and what, in consequence, was their repute in Egypt, which surely is a figure of the world? "Every shepherd is an abomination unto the Egyptians[4]."

But there are three favoured servants of God in particular, special types of the Saviour to come, men raised from low estate to great honour, in whom it was His will that His pastoral office should be thus literally fulfilled. And the first is Jacob, the father of the patriarchs, who appeared before Pharaoh. He became, as Abraham before him, a father of many nations; he "increased exceedingly, and had much cattle, and maid-servants, and men-servants, and camels, and asses[5]," and he was visited by supernatural favours, and had a new name given him—Israel for Jacob. But at the first he was, as his descendants solemnly confessed year

---

[1] Gen. iv. 2. 4.   [2] Luke ii. 8.   [3] Gen. xlvii. 3.
[4] Gen. xlvi. 34.   [5] Gen. xxx. 43.

by year, " a Syrian ready to perish;" and what was his
employment? the care of sheep; and with what toil
and suffering, and for how many years, we learn from
his expostulation with his hard master and relative,
Laban—" This twenty years have I been with thee,"
he says; " thy ewes and thy she-goats have not cast
their young, and the rams of thy flock have I not eaten.
That which was torn of beasts I brought not unto thee;
I bare the loss of it; of my hand didst thou require it,
whether stolen by day, or stolen by night. Thus I was;
in the day the drought consumed me, and the frost by
night; and my sleep departed from mine eyes. Thus
have I been twenty years in thy house; . . . and thou
hast changed my wages ten times [1]."

Who is more favoured than Jacob, who was exalted
to be a Prince with God, and to prevail by intercession?
Yet, you see, he is a shepherd, to image to us that
mystical and true Shepherd and Bishop of souls who
was to come. Yet there is a second and a third as
highly favoured in various ways. The second is Moses,
who drove away the rival shepherds and helped the
daughters of the Priest of Midian to water their flock;
and who, while he was keeping the flock of Jethro, his
father-in-law, saw the Angel of the Lord in a flame of
fire in a bush. And the third is David, the man after
God's own heart. He was " the man who was raised
up on high, the anointed of the God of Jacob, and the

[1] Gen. xxxi. 38—41.

sweet Psalmist of Israel [1];" but he was found among
the sheep. "He took him away from the sheep-folds;
as he was following the ewes great with young ones,
He took him; that he might feed Jacob His people,
and Israel His inheritance. So he fed them with a
faithful and true heart, and ruled them prudently with
all his power [2]." Samuel came to Jesse, and looked
through his seven sons, one by one, but found not him
whom God had chosen: "And Samuel said unto Jesse,
Are here all thy children? And he said, There re-
maineth yet the youngest, and, behold, he keepeth the
sheep." And when he came "he was ruddy, and withal
of a beautiful countenance, and goodly to look to; and
the Lord said, Arise, anoint him, for this is he [3]." And
again, after he had been in Saul's court, he "went and
returned from Saul, to feed his father's sheep at Bethlehem [4];" and when he came to the army his brother
reproached him for "leaving those his few sheep in the
wilderness;" and when he was brought before Saul, he
gave an account how a lion and a bear "took a lamb
out of the flock," and he went after them, and slew
them both, and delivered it. Such were the shepherds
of old times, men at once of peace and of war; men of
simplicity, indeed, "plain men living in tents," "the
meekest of men," yet not easy, indolent men, sitting
in green meadows, and by cool streams, but men of

[1] 2 Sam. xxiii. 1.   [2] Ps. lxxviii. 71—73.
[3] 1 Sam. xvi. 11, 12.   [4] 1 Sam. xvii. 15. 28. 35—37.

rough duties, who were under the necessity to suffer, while they had the opportunity to do exploits.

And if such were the figures, how much more was the Truth itself, the good Shepherd, when He came, both guileless and heroic? If shepherds are men of simple lives and obscure fortunes, uncorrupted and unknown in kings' courts and marts of commerce, how much more He who was "the carpenter's Son," who was "meek and lowly of heart," who "did not strive nor cry," who "went about doing good," who "when He was reviled, reviled not again," and who was "despised and rejected of men"? If, on the other hand, they are men of suffering and trial, how much more so He who was "a man of sorrows," and who "laid down His life for the sheep"?

"That which was torn of beasts I brought not unto thee," says Jacob; "I bare the loss of it; of my hand didst thou require it." And has not Christ undertaken the charge of our souls? Has He not made Himself answerable for us whom the devil had rent? Like the good Samaritan, "Take care of him," He says, "and whatsoever thou spendest more, when I come again I will repay thee[1]." Or, as in another parable, under another image: "Lord, let it alone this year also . . and if it bear fruit, well; and if not, then after that thou shalt cut it down[2]." "In the day the drought consumed me," says Jacob; and who was He who at

[1] Luke x. 35.   [2] Luke xiii. 8, 9.

midday sat down at that very Jacob's well, tired with His journey, and needing some of that water to quench His thirst, whereof "Jacob drank himself, and his children and his cattle"? Yet whereas He had a living water to impart, which the world knew not of, He preferred, as became the good Shepherd, to offer it to one of those lost sheep whom He came to seek and to save, rather than to take at her hand the water from the well, or to accept the offer of His disciples, when they came with meat from the city, and said, "Master, eat." "The frost" consumed me "by night," says Jacob, "and my sleep departed from mine eyes;" and read we not of One whose wont it was to rise a long while before day, and continue in prayer to God? who passed nights in the mountain, or on the sea? who dwelt forty days in the wilderness? who, in the evening and night of His passion, was forlorn in the bleak garden, or stripped and bleeding in the cold judgment hall?

Again: Moses, amid his sheep, saw the vision of God and was told of God's adorable Name; and Christ, the true Shepherd, lived a life of contemplation in the midst of His laborious ministry; He was transfigured on the mountain, and no man knew the Son but the Father, nor the Father but the Son.

Jacob endured, Moses meditated—and David wrought. Jacob endured the frost, and heat, and sleepless nights, and paid the price of the lost sheep; Moses was taken up into the mount for forty days; David fought with the foe, and recovered the prey—he rescued it from the mouth of the lion, and the paw of the bear, and killed the ravenous beasts. Christ, too, not only suffered with Jacob, and was in contemplation with Moses, but fought and conquered with David. David defended his father's sheep at Bethlehem; Christ, born and heralded to the shepherds at Bethlehem, suffered on the Cross in order to conquer. He came "from Edom, with dyed garments from Bozrah[1];" but He was "glorious in His apparel," for He trod the people "in His anger, and trampled them in His fury, and their blood was sprinkled upon His garments, and He stained all His raiment." Jacob was not as David, nor David as Jacob, nor either of them as Moses; but Christ was all three, as fulfilling all types, the lowly Jacob, the wise Moses, the heroic David, all in one—Priest, Prophet, and King.

My brethren, we say daily, "We are His people, and the sheep of His pasture." Again, we say, "We have erred and strayed from Thy ways, like lost sheep:" let us never forget these truths; let us never forget, on the one hand, that we are sinners; let us never forget, on the other hand, that Christ is our Guide and Guardian. He is "the Way, the Truth, and the Life[2]." He is a light unto our ways, and a lanthorn unto our paths. He is our Shepherd, and the sheep know His voice. If we are His sheep, we shall hear it, recognize it, and

[1] Isa. lxiii. 1—3. [2] John xiv. 6.

obey it. Let us beware of not following when He goes before: "He goes before, and His sheep follow Him, for they know His voice." Let us beware of receiving His grace in vain. When God called Samuel, he answered, "Speak, Lord, for Thy servant heareth." When Christ called St. Paul, he "was not disobedient to the heavenly vision." Let us desire to know His voice; let us pray for the gift of watchful ears and a willing heart. He does not call all men in one way; He calls us each in His own way. To St. Peter He said, "Follow thou Me;" of St. John, "If I will that he tarry till I come, what is that to thee?" Nor is it always easy to know His voice. St. John knew it, and said, "It is the Lord," before St. Peter. Samuel did not know it till Eli told him. St. Paul asked, "Who art Thou, Lord?" We are bid, "try the spirits, whether they be of God." But whatever difficulty there be in knowing when Christ calls, and whither, yet at least let us look out for His call. Let us not be content with ourselves; let us not make our own hearts our home, or this world our home, or our friends our home; let us look out for a better country, that is, a heavenly. Let us look out for Him who alone can guide us to that better country; let us call heaven our home, and this life a pilgrimage; let us view ourselves, as sheep in the trackless desert, who, unless they follow the shepherd, will be sure to lose themselves, sure to fall in with the wolf. We are safe while we keep close to Him, and under His eye; but if we suffer Satan to gain an advantage over us, woe to us!

Blessed are they who give the flower of their days, and their strength of soul and body to Him; blessed are they who in their youth turn to Him who gave His life for them, and would fain give it to them and implant it in them, that they may live for ever. Blessed are they who resolve—come good, come evil, come sunshine, come tempest, come honour, come dishonour—that He shall be their Lord and Master, their King and God! They will come to a perfect end, and to peace at the last. They will, with Jacob, confess Him, ere they die, as "the God that fed them all their life long unto that day, the Angel which redeemed them from all evil[1];" with Moses, that "as is their day, so shall their strength be;" and with David, that in "the valley of the shadow of death, they fear no evil, for He is with them, and that His rod and His staff comfort them;" for "when they pass through the waters He will be with them, and through the rivers, they shall not overflow them; when they walk through the fire, they shall not be burnt, neither shall the flame kindle upon them, for He is the Lord their God, the Holy One of Israel, their Saviour."

[1] Gen. xlviii. 15. 16.

SERMON XVII

Religious Joy.[1]

"And the angel said unto them, Fear not: for, behold, I bring you good tidings of great joy, which shall be to all people. For unto you is born this day in the city of David a Saviour, which is Christ the Lord."—LUKE ii. 10, 11.

THERE are two principal lessons which we are taught on the great Festival which we this day celebrate, lowliness and joy. This surely is a day, of all others, in which is set before us the heavenly excellence and the acceptableness in God's sight of that state which most men have, or may have, allotted to them, humble or private life, and cheerfulness in it. If we consult the writings of historians, philosophers, and poets of this world, we shall be led to think great men happy; we shall be led to fix our minds and hearts upon high or conspicuous stations, strange adventures, powerful talents to cope with them, memorable struggles, and great destinies. We shall consider that the highest

---

[1] For Christmas Day.

course of life is the mere pursuit, not the enjoyment of good.

But when we think of this day's Festival, and what we commemorate upon it, a new and very different scene opens upon us. First, we are reminded that though this life must ever be a life of toil and effort, yet that, properly speaking, we have not to seek our highest good. It is found, it is brought near us, in the descent of the Son of God from His Father's bosom to this world. It is stored up among us on earth. No longer need men of ardent minds weary themselves in the pursuit of what they fancy may be chief goods; no longer have they to wander about and encounter peril in quest of that unknown blessedness to which their hearts naturally aspire, as they did in heathen times. The text speaks to them and to all, "Unto you," it says, "is born this day in the city of David a Saviour, which is Christ the Lord."

Nor, again, need we go in quest of any of those things which this vain world calls great and noble. Christ altogether dishonoured what the world esteems, when He took on Himself a rank and station which the world despises. No lot could be more humble and more ordinary than that which the Son of God chose for Himself.

So that we have on the Feast of the Nativity these two lessons—instead of anxiety within and despondence without, instead of a weary search after great things,—to be cheerful and joyful; and, again, to be so in the midst

of those obscure and ordinary circumstances of life
which the world passes over and thinks scorn of.

Let us consider this more at length, as contained in
the gracious narrative of which the text is part.

1. First, what do we read just before the text? that
there were certain shepherds keeping watch over their
flock by night, and Angels appeared to them. Why
should the heavenly hosts appear to these shepherds?
What was it in them which attracted the attention of
the Angels and the Lord of Angels? Were these shepherds learned, distinguished, or powerful? Were they
especially known for piety and gifts? Nothing is said
to make us think so. Faith, we may safely say, they
had, or some of them, for to him that hath more shall be
given; but there is nothing to show that they were
holier and more enlightened than other good men of the
time, who waited for the consolation of Israel. Nay,
there is no reason to suppose that they were better than
the common run of men in their circumstances, simple,
and fearing God, but without any great advances in
piety, or any very formed habits of religion. Why then
were they chosen? for their poverty's sake and obscurity. Almighty God looks with a sort of especial love,
or (as we may term it) affection, upon the lowly. Perhaps it is that man, a fallen, dependent, and destitute
creature, is more in his proper place when he is in lowly
circumstances, and that power and riches, though un-
avoidable in the case of some, are unnatural appendages

to man, as such. Just as there are trades and callings which are unbecoming, though requisite; and while we profit by them, and honour those the more who engage in them, yet we feel we are glad that they are not ours; as we feel grateful and respectful towards a soldier's profession, yet do not affect it; so in God's sight greatness is less acceptable than obscurity. It becomes us less.

The shepherds, then, were chosen on account of their lowliness, to be the first to hear of the Lord's nativity, a secret which none of the princes of this world knew.

And what a contrast is presented to us when we take into account who were our Lord's messengers to them! The Angels who excel in strength, these did His bidding towards the shepherds. Here the highest and the lowest of God's rational creatures are brought together. A set of poor men, engaged in a life of hardship, exposed at that very time to the cold and darkness of the night, watching their flocks, with the view of scaring away beasts of prey or robbers; they—when they are thinking of nothing but earthly things, counting over the tale of their sheep, keeping their dogs by their side, and listening to the noises over the plain, considering the weather and watching for the day—suddenly are met by far other visitants than they conceived. We know the contracted range of thought, the minute and ordinary objects, or rather the one or two objects, to and fro again and again without variety, which engage the minds of men exposed to such a life of heat, cold, and wet, hunger and nakedness, hardship and servitude. They cease to care much for any thing, but go on in a sort of mechanical way, without heart, and still more without reflection.

To men so circumstanced the Angel appeared, to open their minds, and to teach them not to be downcast and in bondage because they were low in the world. He appeared as if to show them that God had chosen the poor in this world to be heirs of His kingdom, and so to do honour to their lot. " Fear not," he said, " for behold I bring you good tidings of great joy, which shall be to all people. For unto you is born this day in the city of David a Saviour, which is Christ the Lord."

2. And now comes a second lesson, which I have said may be gained from the Festival. The Angel honoured a humble lot by his very appearing to the shepherds; next he taught it to be joyful by his message. He disclosed good tidings so much above this world as to equalize high and low, rich and poor, one with another. He said, " Fear not." This is a mode of address frequent in Scripture, as you may have observed, as if man needed some such assurance to support him, especially in God's presence. The Angel said, " Fear not," when he saw the alarm which his presence caused among the shepherds. Even a lesser wonder would have reasonably startled them. Therefore the Angel said, " Fear not." We are naturally afraid of any messenger from the other world, for we have an uneasy conscience when left to

ourselves, and think that his coming forebodes evil. Besides, we so little realize the unseen world, that were Angel or spirit to present himself before us we should be startled by reason of our unbelief, a truth being brought home to our minds which we never apprehended before. So for one or other reason the shepherds were sore afraid when the glory of the Lord shone around about them. And the Angel said, " Fear not." A little religion makes us afraid; when a little light is poured in upon the conscience, there is a darkness visible; nothing but sights of woe and terror; the glory of God alarms while it shines around. His holiness, the range and difficulties of His commandments, the greatness of His power, the faithfulness of His word, frighten the sinner, and men seeing him afraid, think religion has made him so, whereas he is not yet religious at all. They call him religious, when he is merely conscience-stricken. But religion itself, far from inculcating alarm and terror, says, in the words of the Angel, " Fear not;" for such is His mercy, while Almighty God has poured about us His glory, yet it is a consolatory glory, for it is the light of His glory in the Face of Jesus Christ [1]. Thus the heavenly herald tempered the too dazzling brightness of the Gospel on that first Christmas. The glory of God at first alarmed the shepherds, so he added the tidings of good, to work in them a more wholesome and happy temper. Then they rejoiced.

[1] 2 Cor. iv. 6.

"Fear not," said the Angel, "for behold I bring you good tidings of great joy, which shall be to all people. For unto you is born this day in the city of David a Saviour, which is Christ the Lord." And then, when he had finished his announcement, "suddenly there was with the Angel a multitude of the heavenly host, praising God and saying, Glory to God in the highest, and on earth peace, good will towards men." Such were the words which the blessed Spirits who minister to Christ and His Saints, spoke on that gracious night to the shepherds, to rouse them out of their cold and famished mood into great joy; to teach them that they were objects of God's love as much as the greatest of men on earth; nay more so, for to them first He had imparted the news of what that night was happening. His Son was then born into the world. Such events are told to friends and intimates, to those whom we love, to those who will sympathize with us, not to strangers. How could Almighty God be more gracious, and show His favour more impressively to the lowly and the friendless, than by hastening (if I may use the term) to confide the great, the joyful secret to the shepherds keeping watch over their sheep by night?

The Angel then gave the first lesson of mingled humility and joyfulness; but an infinitely greater one was behind in the event itself, to which he directed the shepherds, in that birth itself of the Holy Child Jesus. This he intimated in these words: "Ye shall find the

babe wrapped in swaddling clothes, lying in a manger."
Doubtless, when they heard the Lord's Christ was born
into the world, they would look for Him in kings'
palaces. They would not be able to fancy that He had
become one of themselves, or that they might approach
Him; therefore the Angel thus warned them where to
find Him, not only as a sign, but as a lesson also.

"The shepherds said one to another, Let us now go
even unto Bethlehem, and see this thing which is come
to pass, which the Lord hath made known to us."
Let us too go with them, to contemplate that second
and greater miracle to which the Angel directed them,
the Nativity of Christ. St. Luke says of the Blessed
Virgin, "She brought forth her first-born Son, and
wrapped Him in swaddling clothes, and laid Him in
a manger." What a wonderful sign is this to all the
world, and therefore the Angel repeated it to the shepherds : "Ye shall find the babe wrapped in swaddling
clothes, lying in a manger." The God of heaven and
earth, the Divine Word, who had been in glory with the
Eternal Father from the beginning, He was at this time
born into this world of sin as a little infant. He, as at
this time, lay in His mother's arms, to all appearance
helpless and powerless, and was wrapped by Mary in an
infant's bands, and laid to sleep in a manger. The Son
of God Most High, who created the worlds, became
flesh, though remaining what He was before. He became flesh as truly as if He had ceased to be what

He was, and had actually been changed into flesh.
He submitted to be the offspring of Mary, to be taken
up in the hands of a mortal, to have a mother's eye
fixed upon Him, and to be cherished at a mother's
bosom. A daughter of man became the Mother of God
—to her, indeed, an unspeakable gift of grace; but in
Him what condescension! What an emptying of His
glory to become man! and not only a helpless infant,
though that were humiliation enough, but to inherit all
the infirmities and imperfections of our nature which
were possible to a sinless soul. What were His thoughts,
if we may venture to use such language or admit such
a reflection concerning the Infinite, when human feelings, human sorrows, human wants, first became His?
What a mystery is there from first to last in the Son
of God becoming man! Yet in proportion to the mystery is the grace and mercy of it; and as is the grace,
so is the greatness of the fruit of it.

Let us steadily contemplate the mystery, and say
whether any consequence is too great to follow from
so marvellous a dispensation; any mystery so great,
any grace so overpowering, as that which is already
manifested in the incarnation and death of the Eternal Son. Were we told that the effect of it would
be to make us as Seraphim, that we were to ascend
as high as He descended low—would that startle
us after the Angel's news to the shepherds? And
this indeed is the effect of it, so far as such words

may be spoken without impiety. Men we remain, but not mere men, but gifted with a measure of all those perfections which Christ has in fulness, partaking each in his own degree of His Divine Nature so fully, that the only reason (so to speak) why His saints are not really like Him, is that it is impossible—that He is the Creator, and they His creatures; yet still so, that they are all but Divine, all that they can be made without violating the incommunicable majesty of the Most High. Surely in proportion to His glory is His power of glorifying; so that to say that through Him we shall be made *all but* gods—though it is to say, that we are infinitely below the adorable Creator—still is to say, and truly, that we shall be higher than every other being in the world; higher than Angels or Archangels, Cherubim or Seraphim —that is, not here, or in ourselves, but in heaven and in Christ:—Christ, already the first-fruits of our race, God and man, having ascended high above all creatures, and we through His grace tending to the same high blessedness, having the earnest of His glory given here, and (if we be found faithful) the fulness of it hereafter.

If all these things be so, surely the lesson of joy which the Incarnation gives us is as impressive as the lesson of humility. St. Paul gives us the one lesson in his epistle to the Philippians: " Let this mind be in you, which was also in Christ Jesus: who, being in the form of God, thought it not robbery to be equal with God : but made Himself of no reputation, and took upon Him the form of a servant, and was made in the likeness of men[1]:" and St. Peter gives us the lesson of joyfulness : "whom having not seen, ye love; in whom, though now ye see Him not, yet believing, ye rejoice with joy unspeakable, and full of glory : receiving the end of your faith, even the salvation of your souls."

Take these thoughts with you, my brethren, to your homes on this festive day; let them be with you in your family and social meetings. It is a day of joy : it is good to be joyful—it is wrong to be otherwise. For one day we may put off the burden of our polluted consciences, and rejoice in the perfections of our Saviour Christ, without thinking of ourselves, without thinking of our own miserable uncleanness; but contemplating His glory, His righteousness, His purity, His majesty, His overflowing love. We may rejoice in the Lord, and in all His creatures see Him. We may enjoy His temporal bounty, and partake the pleasant things of earth with Him in our thoughts; we may rejoice in our friends for His sake, loving them most especially because He has loved them.

"God has not appointed us unto wrath, but to obtain salvation through our Lord Jesus Christ, who died for us, that whether we wake or sleep, we should live together with Him." Let us seek the grace of a cheer-

---

[1] Phil. ii. 5—7. 1 Pet. i. 8, 9.

ful heart, an even temper, sweetness, gentleness, and brightness of mind, as walking in His light, and by His grace. Let us pray Him to give us the spirit of ever-abundant, ever-springing love, which overpowers and sweeps away the vexations of life by its own richness and strength, and which above all things unites us to Him who is the fountain and the centre of all mercy, lovingkindness, and joy.

SERMON XVIII.

Ignorance of Evil.

"And the Lord God said, Behold, the man is become as one of Us, to know good and evil."—Gen. iii. 22.

IT is plain that the temptation under which man fell in paradise was this, an ambitious curiosity after knowledge which was not allowed him : next came the desire of the eyes and the flesh, but the forbidden tree was called the tree of *knowledge ;* the Tempter *promised* knowledge ; and after the fall Almighty God pronounced, as in the text, that man had gained it. " Behold, the man is become as one of Us, to *know* good and evil."

You see it is said, " man is become *as one of Us,* to know good and evil," because God does know evil as well as good. This is His wonderful incommunicable attribute ; and man sought to share in what God was, but he could not without ceasing to be what God was also, holy and perfect. It is the incommunicable attribute of God to know evil without experiencing it. But man,

[1] For Innocents' Day.

when he would be as God, could only attain the shadow of a likeness which as yet he had not, by losing the substance which he had already. He shared in God's knowledge by losing His image. God knows evil and is pure from it—man plunged into evil and so knew it.

Our happiness as well as duty lies in not going beyond our measure—in being contented with what we are—with what God makes us. They who seek after forbidden knowledge, of whatever kind, will find they have lost their place in the scale of beings in so doing, and are cast out of the great circle of God's family.

It is, I say, God's incommunicable attribute, as He did not create, so not to experience sin—and as He permits it, so also to know it; to permit it without creating it, to know it without experiencing it—a wonderful and incomprehensible attribute truly, yet involved, perhaps, in the very circumstance that He permits it. For He is every where and in all, and nothing exists except in and through Him. Mysterious as it is, the very prison beneath the earth, its chains and fires and impenitent inmates, the very author of evil himself, is sustained in existence by God, and without God would fall into nothing. God is in hell as well as in heaven, a thought which almost distracts the mind to think of. The awful God! "Whither shall I go from Thy Spirit, or whither shall I go from Thy Presence? If I climb up into heaven, Thou art there; if I go down to hell, Thou art there also." Where life is, there is He; and though it

be but the life of death—the living death of eternal
torment—He is the principle of it. And being thus
intimately present with the very springs of thought,
and the first elements of all being, being the sustaining
cause of all spirits, whether they be good or evil, He is
intimately present *with* evil, being pure from it—and
knows what it is, as being with and in the wretched
atoms which originate it.

If there be this sort of connexion between God's
knowledge and sufferance of evil, see what an ambition
it was in our first parents to desire to know it without
experiencing it; it was, indeed, to desire to be as gods,—
to know the secrets of the prison-house, and to see the
worm that dieth not, yet remain innocent and happy.

This they understood not; they desired something
which they knew not that they could not have, remaining as they were; they did not see how knowledge and
experience went together in the case of human nature;
and Satan did not undeceive them. They ate of the
tree which was to make them wise, and, alas! they saw
clearly what sin was, what shame, what death, what
hell, what despair. They lost God's presence, and they
gained the knowledge of evil. They lost Eden, and
they gained a conscience.

This, in fact, is the knowledge of good and evil.
Lost spirits do not know good. Angels do not know
evil. Beings like ourselves, fallen beings, fallen yet not
cast away, know good and evil; evil not external to

them, nor yet one with them; but in them, yet not simply of them. Such was the fruit of the forbidden tree, as it remains in us to this day.

We do not know in what the duty and happiness of other beings consist; but at least this seems to have been man's happiness in Paradise, not to think about himself or to be conscious of himself. Such, too, to recur to the parallel especially suggested on this day, seems to be the state of children. They do not reflect upon themselves. Such, too, seems to be the state of those orders of Angels whose life is said to consist in contemplation—for what is contemplation but a resting in the thought of God to the forgetfulness of self? Hence the Saints are described as "Virgins who *follow the Lamb whithersoever He goeth.*" But Adam, discontented with what he was, pined after a knowledge which he could not obtain from without—which he could only have from miserable experience within—from moral disorders within him, and from having his mind drawn to the contemplation of himself in consequence of those disorders. He obtained the wished for knowledge; and his first recorded act afterwards was one of reflection upon self, and he hid himself among the trees of the garden. He was no longer fitted for contemplating glories without him; his attention was arrested to the shame that was upon him.

What is so miserably seen in the history of our first parents has been the temptation and sin of their posterity

s 2

ever since,—indulgence in forbidden, unlawful, hurtful, unprofitable knowledge; as some instances will show.

1. I ought to notice in the first place that evil curiosity which stimulates young persons to intrude into things of which it is their blessedness to be ignorant. Satan gains our souls step by step; and his first allurement is the knowledge of what is wrong. He first tempts them to the knowledge, and then to the commission of sin. Depend on it that our happiness and our glory, in these matters, is to be ignorant, as well as to be guiltless. St. Paul says that " it is a shame even to speak " of those things which are done by the sons of Belial in secret. Oh, thoughtless, and worse, oh, cruel to your own selves, all ye who read what ye should not read, and hear what ye should not hear! Oh, how will you repent of your folly afterwards! Oh, what bitter feelings, oh, what keen pangs, will shoot through your souls hereafter, at the memory, when you look back, of what has come of that baneful curiosity! Oh, how will you despise yourselves, oh, how weep at what you have brought on you! At this day surely there is a special need of this warning; for this is a day when nothing is not pried into, nothing is not published, nothing is not laid before all men.

2. In the next place I would observe, that the pursuit of science, which characterizes these times, is very likely to draw us aside into a sin of a particular kind, if we are not on our guard. We read, in the book of Acts, of

many who used curious arts burning their books; that is, there are kinds of knowledge which are forbidden to the Christian. Now this seems strange to the world in this day. The only forbidden subjects which they can fancy, are such as are not *true*—fictions, impostures, superstitions, and the like. Falsehood they think wrong; false religions, for instance, *because* false. But they are perplexed when told that there may be branches of real knowledge, yet forbidden. Yet it has ever been considered in the Church, as in Scripture, that soothsaying, consulting the stars, magic, and similar arts, are unlawful—unlawful, even though not false; and Scripture certainly speaks as if at least some of them were more than merely a pretended knowledge and a pretended power; whereas men now-a-days have got to think that they are wrong, merely because *frauds* and *impostures;* and if they found them not so, they would be very slow to understand how still they are unlawful. They have not mastered the idea that real knowledge may be forbidden us.

3. Next it is obvious to speak of those melancholy persons who boast themselves on what they call their knowledge of the world and of life. There are men, alas not a few, who look upon acquaintance with evil as if a part of their education. Instead of shunning vice and sin, they try it, if for no other reason, simply for this— that they may have knowledge of it. They mix with various classes of men, and they throw themselves into

[VIII]   S 2 the manners and opinions of all in turn. They are ready-witted perhaps, prompt and versatile, and easily adapt themselves so as to please and get acquainted with those they fall in with. They have no scruples of conscience hindering them from complying with whatever is proposed; they are of any form of religion, have lax or correct morals, according to the occasion. They can revel with those that revel, and they can speak serious things when their society is serious. They travel up and down the country perhaps, or they are of professions or pursuits which introduce them to men of various languages, or which take them abroad, and they see persons of opposite creeds and principles, and whatever they fall in with they take as so many facts, merely as facts of human nature, not as things right or wrong according to a certain fixed standard independent of themselves. Now whatever of religion or truth remains in our fallen nature is not on the surface: these men, then, studying what is uppermost, are in fact but studying all that is evil in man, and in consequence they have very low notions of man. They are very sceptical about the existence of principle and virtue; they think all men equally swayed by worldly, selfish, or sensual motives, though some hide their motives better than others, or have feelings and likings of a more refined character. And having given in to sin themselves, they have no higher principle within them to counteract the effect of what they see without; all their notions of man's nature, capabilities, and destinies, are derived from, and are measured by, what goes on in the world, and accordingly they apply all their knowledge to bad purposes. They think they know, and they do know too truly on the whole, the motives and inducements which will prevail with men; and they use their knowledge to overreach, deceive, seduce, corrupt, or sway those with whom they have to do.

4. Another very different class of persons who study evil, and pride themselves upon it, and are degraded by it, are those who indulge themselves in contemplating and dwelling on the struggle between right and wrong in their own minds. There have been from time to time men of morbid imaginations, of any or no religious creed, who have so exercised themselves. Indeed there has been a large school of writers in very various departments, for years, I may say centuries past, though happily they are diminishing now, who delight in bringing out into open day all the weaknesses and inconsistencies of human nature; nay worse, take pains to describe bad men, and how they feel, and what they say; who interest the mind in bad men, nay in bad Angels, as if Satan might be thought of otherwise than with shuddering. And there are others, men of mistaken religious views, who think that religion consists in dwelling on and describing the struggle between grace and corrupt nature in the soul. Christ has brought us light and life, and would have us put off what we are,

and follow Him, who knew no sin. But these men, far from rising even to the aspiration after perfection, do not advance in their notion of spiritual religion beyond the idea of declaring and lamenting their want of it. Confession is with them perfection; nay, it is almost the test of a Christian, to be able to discourse upon his inward corruption. It is well to confess sin in detail with shame as an act of penitence; it is a snare to speak of it vaguely and in public.

5. Lastly, even when used rightly, the knowledge of sin is not without its danger. As mediciners would not exist were there no illness or disease, so it is mental disease which gives rise to casuists. Pain leads us to think of our bodies, and sin of our souls. Were our souls in perfect harmony, they would act like an instrument in tune; we should with difficulty divide the sounds, even if we would; but it is the discordance, the jar within us, which leads us to a serious contemplation of what we are. The same remark obviously applies to a great deal of theological knowledge, on which men who have it are tempted to pride themselves; I mean exact knowledge of heresies and the like. The love of God alone can give such knowledge its right direction. There is the danger lest men so informed find themselves scrutinizing when they should be adoring, reasoning when they should be believing, comparing when they should be choosing, and proving when they should be acting. We know two things of the

Angels—that they cry Holy, Holy, Holy, and that they
do God's bidding. Worship and service make up their
blessedness; and such is our blessedness in proportion as
we approach them. But all exercises of mind which lead
us to reflect upon and ascertain our state; to know what
worship is, and why we worship; what service is, and
why we serve; what our feelings imply, and what our
words mean, tend to divert our minds from the one thing
needful, unless we are practised and expert in using them.
All proofs of religion, evidences, proofs of particular doctrines, scripture proofs, and the like,—these certainly fur-
nish scope for the exercise of great and admirable powers
of mind, and it would be fanatical to disparage or disown
them; but it requires a mind rooted and grounded in
love not to be dissipated by them. As for truly religious
minds, they, when so engaged, instead of mere disputing,
are sure to turn inquiry into meditation, exhortation
into worship, and argument into teaching.

Reflections such as these, followed up, show us how
different is our state from that for which God made us.
He meant us to be simple, and we are unreal; He
meant us to think no evil, and a thousand associations,
bad, trifling, or unworthy, attend our every thought.
He meant us to be drawn on to the glories without us,
and we are drawn back and (as it were) fascinated by
the miseries within us. And hence it is that the whole
structure of society is so artificial; no one trusts another,

if he can help it; safeguards, checks, and securities are
ever sought after.   No one means exactly what he says,
for our words have lost their natural meaning, and even
an Angel could not use them naturally, for every mind
being different from every other, they have no distinct
meaning.   What, indeed, is the very function of society,
as it is at present, but a rude attempt to cover the
degradation of the fall, and to make men feel respect for
themselves, and enjoy it in the eyes of others, without
returning to God.   This is what we should especially
guard against, because there is so much of it in the
world.   I mean, not an abandonment of evil, not a
sweeping away and cleansing out of the corruption
which sin has bred within us, but a smoothing it over,
an outside delicacy and polish, an ornamenting the
surface of things while " within are dead men's bones
and all uncleanness;" making the garments, which at
first were given for decency, a means of pride and
vanity.   Men give good names to what is evil, they
sanctify bad principles and feelings; and, knowing that
there is vice and error, selfishness, pride, and ambition,
in the world, they attempt, not to root out these evils,
not to withstand these errors;—that they think a
dream, the dream of theorists who do not know the
world;—but to cherish and form alliance with them,
to use them, to make a science of selfishness, to flatter
and indulge error, and to bribe vice with the promise
of bearing with it, so that it does but keep in the shade.

But let us, finding ourselves in the state in which we are, take those means which alone are really left us, which alone become us. Adam, when he had sinned, and felt himself fallen, instead of honestly abandoning what he had become, would fain have hid himself. He went a step further. He did not give up what he now was, partly from dread of God, partly from dislike of what he had been. He had learnt to love sin and to fear God's justice. But Christ has purchased for us what we lost in Adam, our garment of innocence. He has bid us and enabled us to become as little children; He has purchased for us the grace of *simplicity*, which, though one of the highest, is very little thought about, is very little sought after. We have, indeed, a general idea what love is, and hope, and faith, and truth, and purity, though a poor idea; but we are almost blind to what is one of the first elements of Christian perfection, that simple-mindedness which springs from the heart's being *whole* with God, entire, undivided. And those who think they have an idea of it, commonly rise no higher than to mistake for it a mere weakness and softness of mind, which is but its counterfeit. To be simple is to be like the Apostles and first Christians. Our Saviour says, " Be ye harmless," or simple, " as doves." And St. Paul, " I would have you wise unto that which is good, and *simple concerning evil*[1]." Again, " That ye may be *blameless and harmless*, the sons of

[1] Rom. xvi. 19.

God, without rebuke, in the midst of a crooked and perverse nation[1]." And he speaks of the "testimony of"
his own "conscience, that in *simplicity* and godly sincerity, not with fleshly wisdom, but by the grace of God,"
he had his conversation in the world and towards his
disciples. Let us pray God to give us this great and
precious gift; that we may blot out from our memory
all that offends Him; unlearn all that knowledge which
sin has taught us; rid ourselves of selfish motives, self-
conceit, and vanity, littlenesses, envying, grudgings,
meannesses; turn from all cowardly, low, miserable
ways; and escape from servile fears, the fear of man,
vague anxieties of conscience, and superstitions. So
that we may have the boldness and frankness of those
who are as if they had no sin, from having been cleansed
from it; the uncontaminated hearts, open countenances,
and untroubled eyes of those who neither suspect, nor
conceal, nor shun, nor are jealous; in a word, so that
we may have confidence in Him, that we may stay on
Him, and rest in the thoughts of Him, instead of plung-
ing amid the thickets of this world; that we may bear
His eye and His voice, and know no knowledge but
the knowledge of Him and Jesus Christ crucified, and
desire no objects but what He has blessed and bid us
pursue.

[1] Phil. ii. 16.

END OF VOL. VIII.

A

SELECT LIST OF WORKS

PUBLISHED BY

LONGMANS, GREEN, & CO.

LONDON AND NEW YORK.

MESSRS. LONGMANS, GREEN, & CO.

Issue the undermentioned Lists of their Publications, which may be had post free on application to them at 39 Paternoster Row, London, E.C.:

1. MONTHLY LIST OF NEW WORKS AND NEW EDITIONS.

2. QUARTERLY LIST OF ANNOUNCEMENTS AND NEW WORKS.

3. NOTES ON BOOKS: BEING AN ANALYSIS OF THE WORKS PUBLISHED DURING EACH QUARTER.

4. CATALOGUE OF SCIENTIFIC WORKS.

5. CATALOGUE OF MEDICAL AND SURGICAL WORKS.

6. CATALOGUE OF SCHOOL BOOKS AND EDUCATIONAL WORKS.

7. CATALOGUE OF BOOKS FOR ELEMENTARY SCHOOLS AND PUPIL TEACHERS.

8. CATALOGUE OF THEOLOGICAL WORKS BY DIVINES AND MEMBERS OF THE CHURCH OF ENGLAND.

9. CATALOGUE OF WORKS IN GENERAL LITERATURE.

CARDINAL NEWMAN'S WORKS.

Parochial and Plain Sermons. Edited by REV. W. J. COPELAND, B.D., late Rector of Farnham, Essex. 8 vols. Sold separately. Crown 8vo. Cabinet Edition, 5s. each; Popular Edition, 3s. 6d. each.

CONTENTS OF VOL. I.:—Holiness necessary for Future Blessedness—The Immortality of the Soul—Knowledge of God's Will without Obedience—Secret Faults—Self-Denial the Test of Religious Earnestness—The Spiritual Mind—Sins of Ignorance and Weakness—God's Commandments not Grievous—The Religious Use of Excited Feelings—Profession without Practice—Profession without Hypocrisy—Profession without Ostentation—Promising without Doing—Religious Emotion—Religious Faith Rational—The Christian Mysteries—The Self-Wise Inquirer—Obedience the Remedy for Religious Perplexity—Times of Private Prayer—Forms of Private Prayer—The Resurrection of the Body—Witnesses of the Resurrection—Christian Reverence—The Religion of the Day—Scripture a Record of Human Sorrow—Christian Manhood.

CONTENTS OF VOL. II.:—The World's Benefactors—Faith without Sight—The Incarnation—Martyrdom—Love of Relations and Friends—The Mind of Little Children—Ceremonies of the Church—The Glory of the Christian Church—St. Paul's Conversion viewed in Reference to his Office—Secrecy and Suddenness of Divine Visitations—Divine Decrees—The Reverence Due to the Blessed Virgin Mary—Christ, a Quickening Spirit—Saving Knowledge—Self-Contemplation—Religious Cowardice—The Gospel Witnesses—Mysteries in Religion—The Indwelling Spirit—The Kingdom of the Saints—The Gospel, a Trust Committed to us—Tolerance of Religious Error—Rebuking Sin—The Christian Ministry—Human Responsibility—Guilelessness—The Danger of Riches—The Powers of Nature—The Danger of Accomplishments—Christian Zeal—Use of Saints' Days.

CARDINAL NEWMAN'S WORKS.

Parochial and Plain Sermons.—*Continued.*

CONTENTS OF VOL. III.:—Abraham and Lot—Wilfulness of Israel in Rejecting Samuel—Saul—Early Years of David—Jeroboam—Faith and Obedience—Christian Repentance—Contracted Views in Religion—A particular Providence as revealed in the Gospel—Tears of Christ at the Grave of Lazarus—Bodily Suffering—The Humiliation of the Eternal Son—Jewish Zeal a Pattern to Christians—Submission to Church Authority—Contest between Truth and Falsehood in the Church—The Church Visible and Invisible—The Visible Church an Encouragement to Faith—The Gift of the Spirit—Regenerating Baptism—Infant Baptism—The Daily Service—The Good Part of Mary—Religious Worship a Remedy for Excitements—Intercession—The Intermediate State.

CONTENTS OF VOL. IV.:—The Strictness of the Law of Christ—Obedience without Love, as instanced in the Character of Balaam—Moral Consequences of Single Sins—Acceptance of Religious Privileges Compulsory—Reliance on Religious Observances—The Individuality of the Soul—Chastisement amid Mercy—Peace and Joy amid Chastisement—The State of Grace—The Visible Church for the Sake of the Elect—The Communion of Saints—The Church a Home for the Lonely—The Invisible World—The Greatness and Littleness of Human Life—Moral Effects of Communion with God—Christ Hidden from the World—Christ Manifested in Remembrance—The Gainsaying of Korah—The Mysteriousness of our Present Being—The Ventures of Faith—Faith and Love—Watching—Keeping Fast and Festival.

CONTENTS OF VOL. V.:—Worship, a Preparation for Christ's Coming—Reverence, a Belief in God's Presence—Unreal Words—Shrinking from Christ's Coming—Equanimity—Remembrance of Past Mercies—The Mystery of Godliness—The State of Innocence—Christian Sympathy—Righteousness not of us, but in us—The Law of the Spirit—The New Works of the Gospel—The State of Salvation—Transgressions and Infirmities—Sins of Infirmity—Sincerity and Hypocrisy—The Testimony of Conscience—Many called, Few chosen—Present Blessings—Endurance, the Christian's Portion—Affliction, a School of Comfort—The Thought of God, the Stay of the Soul—Love, the One Thing Needful—The Power of the Will.

CONTENTS OF VOL. VI.:—Fasting, a Source of Trial—Life, the Season of Repentance—Apostolic Abstinence, a Pattern for Christians—Christ's Privations, a Meditation for Christians—Christ the Son of God made Man—The Incarnate Son, a Sufferer and Sacrifice—The Cross of Christ the Measure of the World—Difficulty of realising Sacred Privileges—The Gospel Sign Addressed to Faith—The Spiritual Presence of Christ in the Church—The Eucharistic Presence—Faith the Title for Justification—Judaism of the Present Day—The Fellowship of the Apostles—Rising with Christ—Warfare the Condition of Victory—Waiting for Christ—Subjection of the Reason and Feelings to the Revealed Word—The Gospel Palaces—The Visible Temple—Offerings for the Sanctuary—The Weapons of Saints—Faith Without Demonstration—The Mystery of the Holy Trinity—Peace in Believing.

CONTENTS OF VOL. VII.:—The Lapse of Time—Religion, a Weariness to the Natural Man—The World our Enemy—The Praise of Men—Temporal Advantages—The Season of Epiphany—The Duty of Self-Denial—The Yoke of Christ—Moses the Type of Christ—The Crucifixion—Attendance on Holy Communion—The Gospel Feast—Love of Religion, a new Nature—Religion Pleasant to the Religious—Mental Prayer—Infant Baptism—The Unity of the Church—Steadfastness in the Old Paths.

CONTENTS OF VOL. VIII.:—Reverence in Worship—Divine Calls—The Trial of Saul—The Call of David—Curiosity, a Temptation to Sin—Miracles no Remedy for Unbelief—Josiah, a Pattern for the Ignorant—Inward Witness to the Truth of the Gospel—Jeremiah, a Lesson for the Disappointed—Endurance of the World's Censure—Doing Glory to God in Pursuits of the World—Vanity of Human Glory—Truth Hidden when not Sought after—Obedience to God the Way to Faith in Christ—Sudden Conversions—The Shepherd of our Souls—Religious Joy—Ignorance of Evil.

Sermons Preached on Various Occasions.   Crown 8vo.   Cabinet Edition, 6s. ; Popular Edition, 3s. 6d.

CONTENTS :—Intellect the Instrument of Religious Training—The Religion of the Pharisee and the Religion of Mankind—Waiting for Christ—The Secret Power of Divine Grace—Dispositions for Faith—Omnipotence in Bonds—St. Paul's Characteristic Gift—St. Paul's Gift of Sympathy—Christ upon the Waters—The Second Spring—Order, the Witness and Instrument of Unity—The Mission of St. Philip Neri—The Tree beside the Waters—In the World, but not of the World—The Pope and the Revolution.

CARDINAL NEWMAN'S WORKS.

Selection, Adapted to the Seasons of the Ecclesiastical Year,
from the 'Parochial and Plain Sermons.' Edited by the REV. W.
J. COPELAND, B.D. Crown 8vo. Cabinet Edition, 5s.; Popular
Edition, 3s. 6d.

CONTENTS :—*Advent:* Self-Denial the Test of Religious Earnestness—Divine Calls—
The Ventures of Faith—Watching. *Christmas Day:* Religious Joy. *New Year's Sunday:*
The Lapse of Time. *Epiphany:* Remembrance of Past Mercies—Equanimity—The
Immortality of the Soul—Christian Manhood—Sincerity and Hypocrisy—Christian
Sympathy. *Septuagesima:* Present Blessings. *Sexagesima:* Endurance, the Christian's
Portion. *Quinquagesima:* Love, the One Thing Needful. *Lent:* The Individuality of the
Soul—Life the Season of Repentance—Bodily Suffering—Tears of Christ at the Grave of
Lazarus—Christ's Privations, a Meditation for Christians—The Cross of Christ the Measure
of the World. *Good Friday:* The Crucifixion. *Easter Day:* Keeping Fast and Festival.
Easter Tide: Witnesses of the Resurrection—A Particular Providence as Revealed in the
Gospel—Christ Manifested in Remembrance—The Invisible World—Waiting for Christ.
Ascension: Warfare the Condition of Victory. *Sunday after Ascension:* Rising with
Christ. *Whitsun Day:* The Weapons of Saints. *Trinity Sunday:* The Mysteriousness
of Our Present Being. *Sundays after Trinity:* Holiness Necessary for Future Blessedness
—The Religious Use of Excited Feelings—The Self-Wise Inquirer—Scripture a Record of
Human Sorrow—The Danger of Riches—Obedience without Love, as instanced in the
Character of Balaam—Moral Consequences of Single Sins—The Greatness and Littleness
of Human Life—Moral Effects of Communion with God—The Thought of God the Stay of
the Soul—The Power of the Will—The Gospel Palaces—Religion a Weariness to the
Natural Man—The World our Enemy—The Praise of Men—Religion Pleasant to the
Religious—Mental Prayer—Curiosity a Temptation to Sin—Miracles no Remedy for Unbelief—Jeremiah, a Lesson for the Disappointed—The Shepherd of our Souls—Doing Glory
to God in Pursuits of the World.

Sermons Bearing upon Subjects of the Day. Edited by the REV.
W. J. COPELAND, B.D., late Rector of Farnham, Essex. Crown
8vo. Cabinet Edition, 5s.; Popular Edition, 3s. 6d.

CONTENTS :—The Work of the Christian—Saintliness not Forfeited by the Penitent—
Our Lord's Last Supper and His First—Dangers to the Penitent—The Three Offices of
Christ—Faith and Experience—Faith unto the World—The Church and the World—In-
dulgence in Religious Privileges—Connection between Personal and Public Improvement
—Christian Nobleness—Joshua a Type of Christ and His Followers—Elisha a Type of
Christ and His Followers—The Christian Church a Continuation of the Jewish—The
Principles of Continuity between the Jewish and Christian Churches—The Christian
Church an Imperial Power—Sanctity the Token of the Christian Empire—Condition of the
Members of the Christian Empire—The Apostolic Christian—Wisdom and Innocence—
Invisible Presence of Christ—Outward and Inward Notes of the Church—Grounds for
Steadfastness in our Religious Profession—Elijah the Prophet of the Latter Days—Feast-
ing in Captivity—The Parting of Friends.

Fifteen Sermons Preached before the University of Oxford,
between A.D. 1826 and 1843. Crown 8vo. Cabinet Edition, 5s.;
Popular Edition, 3s. 6d.

CONTENTS :—The Philosophical Temper, first enjoined by the Gospel—The Influence of
Natural and Revealed Religion respectively—Evangelical Sanctity the Perfection of
Natural Virtue—The Usurpations of Reason—Personal Influence, the Means of Propagating
the Truth—On Justice as a Principle of Divine Governance—Contest between Faith
and Sight—Human Responsibility, as independent of Circumstances—Wilfulness, the Sin
of Saul—Faith and Reason, contrasted as Habits of Mind—The Nature of Faith in Relation
to Reason—Love, the Safeguard of Faith against Superstition—Implicit and Explicit
Reason—Wisdom, as contrasted with Faith and with Bigotry—The Theory of Develop-
ments in Religious Doctrine.

CARDINAL NEWMAN'S WORKS.

Discourses Addressed to Mixed Congregations. Crown 8vo. Cabinet Edition, 5s.; Popular Edition, 3s. 6d.

CONTENTS :—The Salvation of the Hearer the Motive of the Preacher—Neglect of Divine Calls and Warnings—Men not Angels—The Priests of the Gospel—Purity and Love—Saintliness the Standard of Christian Principle—God's Will the End of Life—Perseverance in Grace—Nature and Grace—Illuminating Grace—Faith and Private Judgment—Faith and Doubt—Prospects of the Catholic Missioner—Mysteries of Nature and of Grace—The Mystery of Divine Condescension—The Infinitude of Divine Attributes—Mental Sufferings of Our Lord in His Passion—The Glories of Mary for the Sake of Her Son—On the Fitness of the Glories of Mary.

Lectures on the Doctrine of Justification. Crown 8vo. Cabinet Edition, 5s. ; Popular Edition, 3s. 6d.

CONTENTS :—Faith considered as the Instrumental Cause of Justification—Love considered as the Formal Cause of Justification—Primary Sense of the term 'Justification'—Secondary Senses of the term 'Justification'—Misuse of the term 'Just' or 'Righteous'—The Gift of Righteousness—The Characteristics of the Gift of Righteousness—Righteousness viewed as a Gift and as a Quality—Righteousness the Fruit of our Lord's Resurrection—The Office of Justifying Faith—The Nature of Justifying Faith—Faith viewed relatively to Rites and Works—On Preaching the Gospel—Appendix.

On the Development of Christian Doctrine. Crown 8vo. Cabinet Edition, 6s.; Popular Edition, 3s. 6d.

On the Idea of a University. Crown 8vo. Cabinet Edition, 7s.; Popular Edition, 3s. 6d.

An Essay in Aid of a Grammar of Assent. Crown 8vo. Cabinet Edition, 7s. 6d.; Popular Edition, 3s. 6d.

Two Essays on Miracles. 1. Of Scripture. 2. Of Ecclesiastical History. Crown 8vo. Cabinet Edition, 6s. ; Popular Edition, 3s. 6d.

Discussions and Arguments. Crown 8vo. Cabinet Edition, 6s.; Popular Edition, 3s. 6d.

1. How to accomplish it. 2. The Antichrist of the Fathers. 3. Scripture and the Creed. 4. Tamworth Reading-room. 5. Who's to Blame? 6. An Argument for Christianity.

Essays, Critical and Historical. 2 vols. Crown 8vo. Cabinet Edition, 12s.; Popular Edition, 7s.

1. Poetry. 2. Rationalism. 3. Apostolic Tradition. 4. De la Mennais. 5. Palmer on Faith and Unity. 6. St. Ignatius. 7. Prospects of the Anglican Church. 8. The Anglo-American Church. 9. Countess of Huntingdon. 10. Catholicity of the Anglican Church. 11. The Antichrist of Protestants. 12. Milman's Christianity. 13. Reformation of the XI. Century. 14. Private Judgment. 15. Davison. 16. Keble.

CARDINAL NEWMAN'S WORKS.

Apologia Pro Vita Sua. Crown 8vo. Cabinet Edition, 6s. ; Popular Edition, 3s. 6d.

Verses on Various Occasions. Crown 8vo. Cabinet Edition, 6s. ; Popular Edition, 3s. 6d.

Historical Sketches. 3 vols. Crown 8vo. Cabinet Edition, 6s. each; Popular Edition, 3s. 6d. each.

1. The Turks. 2. Cicero. 3. Apollonius. 4. Primitive Christianity. 5. Church of the Fathers. 6. St. Chrysostom. 7. Theodoret. 8. St. Benedict. 9. Benedictine Schools. 10. Universities. 11. Northmen and Normans. 12. Mediæval Oxford. 13. Convocation of Canterbury.

The Arians of the Fourth Century. Crown 8vo. Cabinet Edition, 6s.; Popular Edition, 3s. 6d.

Select Treatises of St. Athanasius in Controversy with the Arians. Freely translated. 2 vols. Crown 8vo. Cabinet Edition, 15s.

Theological Tracts. Crown 8vo. Cabinet Edition, 8s.

1. Dissertatiunculæ. 2. On the Text of the Seven Epistles of St. Ignatius. 3. Doctrinal Causes of Arianism. 4. Apollinarianism. 5. St. Cyril's Formula. 6. Ordo de Tempore. 7. Douay Version of Scriptures.

The Via Media of the Anglican Church. 2 vols. Crown 8vo. Cabinet Edition, 6s. each ; Popular Edition, 3s. 6d. each.
Vol. I. Prophetical Office of the Church.
Vol. II. Occasional Letters and Tracts.

Certain Difficulties felt by Anglicans in Catholic Teaching Considered. 2 vols.
Vol. I. Twelve Lectures. Crown 8vo. Cabinet Edition, 7s. 6d.; Popular Edition, 3s. 6d.
Vol. II. Letters to Dr. Pusey concerning the Blessed Virgin, and to the Duke of Norfolk in defence of the Pope and Council. Crown 8vo. Cabinet Edition, 5s. 6d. ; Popular Edition, 3s. 6d.

Present Position of Catholics in England. Crown 8vo. Cabinet Edition, 7s. 6d. ; Popular Edition, 3s. 6d.

Loss and Gain. The Story of a Convert. Crown 8vo. Cabinet Edition, 6s. ; Popular Edition, 3s. 6d.

Callista. A Tale of the Third Century. Crown 8vo. Cabinet Edition, 6s. ; Popular Edition, 3s. 6d.

The Dream of Gerontius. 16mo, sewed, 6d.; cloth, 1s.

CARDINAL NEWMAN'S WORKS.

POPULAR EDITION.

Parochial and Plain Sermons. 8 vols. Each	3s. 6d.
Sermons preached on Various Occasions	3s. 6d.
Selection, from the Parochial and Plain Sermons	3s. 6d.
Sermons bearing on Subjects of the Day	3s. 6d.
Sermons preached before the University of Oxford	3s. 6d.
Discourses addressed to Mixed Congregations	3s. 6d.
Lectures on the Doctrine of Justification	3s. 6d.
On the Development of Christian Doctrine	3s. 6d.
On the Idea of a University	3s. 6d.
An Essay in Aid of a Grammar of Assent	3s. 6d.
Biblical and Ecclesiastical Miracles	3s. 6d.
Discussions and Arguments on Various Subjects	3s. 6d.
Essays, Critical and Historical. 2 vols. Each	3s. 6d.
Historical Sketches. 3 vols. Each	3s. 6d.
The Arians of the Fourth Century	3s. 6d.
The Via Media of the Anglican Church. 2 vols. Each	3s. 6d.
Difficulties felt by Anglicans considered. 2 vols. Each	3s. 6d.
Present Position of Catholics in England	3s. 6d.
Apologia pro Vita Sua	3s. 6d.
Verses on Various Occasions	3s. 6d.
Loss and Gain	3s. 6d.
Callista	3s. 6d.

BARRAUD.—**Saint Thomas of Canterbury and Saint Elizabeth of Hungary** : Historical Dramas. By CLEMENT WILLIAM BARRAUD, S.J. Crown 8vo. 5s.

FOUARD.—**The Christ, The Son of God.** A Life of Our Lord and Saviour Jesus Christ. By the ABBÉ CONSTANT FOUARD, Honorary Cathedral Canon, Professor of the Faculty of Theology at Rouen, etc., etc. Translated from the Fifth Edition with the Author's sanction. By GEORGE F. X. GRIFFITH. With an Introduction by CARDINAL MANNING. Third Edition. With 3 Maps. 2 vols. Crown 8vo. 14s.

'In erudition the author is to the full up to the level of any writers, Catholic or Protestant, who have as yet attempted the same task, while his reliableness in matters of dogma gives him an enormous scientific advantage over non-Catholics.'—*Dublin Review.*

Saint Peter and the First Years of Christianity. By the ABBÉ CONSTANT FOUARD. Translated by GEORGE F. X. GRIFFITH. Crown 8vo. 9s.

LYONS.—Christianity or Infallibility—Both or Neither. By the
Rev. DANIEL LYONS. Crown 8vo. 5s.

'His method is thoroughly popular, and while he has admirably succeeded in avoiding
that didactic and argumentative style which is apt to repel the ordinary reader of our
day, he nevertheless leaves the distinct impression that his reasoning is based on sound
logic, and strengthened by such authorities as would command the attention of every
theological student.

'The work is full of erudition, as is shown by the numerous notes indicating a wide
range of pertinent and careful reading. . . . The book is a solid and timely contribution
to the theological literature of the day.'—*American Ecclesiastical Review.*

CLARKE.—A Pilgrimage to the Holy Coat of Treves. With
an Account of its History and Authenticity. By RICHARD F.
CLARKE, S.J. With Illustrations. Crown 8vo. 4s.

CHRISTIAN BIOGRAPHIES:

Henri Dominique Lacordaire. A Biographical Sketch. By
H. L. SIDNEY LEAR. With Frontispiece. Crown 8vo. 3s. 6d.

A Christian Painter of the Nineteenth Century; being the
Life of Hippolyte Flandrin. By H. L. SIDNEY LEAR. Crown
8vo. 3s. 6d.

Bossuet and his Contemporaries. By H. L. SIDNEY LEAR.
Crown 8vo. 3s. 6d.

Fénelon, Archbishop of Cambrai. A Biographical Sketch. By
H. L. SIDNEY LEAR. Crown 8vo. 3s. 6d.

A Dominican Artist. A Sketch of the Life of the Rev. Père
Besson, of the Order of St. Dominic. By H. L. SIDNEY LEAR.
Crown 8vo. 3s. 6d.

The Life of Madame Louise de France, Daughter of Louis XV.,
also known as the Mother Thérèse de S. Augustin. By H. L.
SIDNEY LEAR. Crown 8vo. 3s. 6d.

The Revival of Priestly Life in the Seventeenth Century in
France. Charles de Condren—S. Philip Neri and Cardinal de
Berulle—S. Vincent de Paul—S. Sulpice and Jean Jacques Olier.
By H. L. SIDNEY LEAR. Crown 8vo. 3s. 6d.

Life of S. Francis de Sales, Bishop and Prince of Geneva. By H.
L. SIDNEY LEAR. Crown 8vo. 3s. 6d.

Henri Perreyve. By A. GRATRY, PRÊTRE DE L'ORATOIRE,
Professeur de Morale Evangélique à la Sorbonne, et Membre de
l'Académie Française. Translated, by special permission, by H.
L. SIDNEY LEAR. With Portrait. Crown 8vo. 3s. 6d.

FÉNELON.—Spiritual Letters to Men. By ARCHBISHOP FÉNELON. Translated by H. L. SIDNEY LEAR, author of 'Life of Fénelon,' 'Life of S. Francis de Sales,' etc. etc. 16mo. 2s. 6d.

Spiritual Letters to Women.—By ARCHBISHOP FÉNELON. Translated by H. L. SIDNEY LEAR, author of 'Life of Fénelon,' 'Life of S. Francis de Sales,' etc. etc. 16mo. 2s. 6d.

DRANE.— The History of St. Dominic, Founder of the Friar Preachers. By AUGUSTA THEODORA DRANE, author of 'The History of St. Catherine of Siena and her Companions.' With 32 Illustrations. 8vo. 15s.

JAMESON—Works by MRS. JAMESON :

Sacred and Legendary Art. With 19 Etchings and 197 Woodcuts. 2 vols. Cloth, gilt top. 20s. *net.*

Legends of the Madonna : The Virgin Mary as Represented in Sacred and Legendary Art. With 27 Etchings and 165 Woodcuts. 1 vol. Cloth, gilt top. 10s. *net.*

Legends of the Monastic Orders. With 11 Etchings and 88 Woodcuts. 1 vol. Cloth, gilt top. 10s. *net.*

History of the Saviour, His Types and Precursors. Completed by LADY EASTLAKE. With 13 Etchings and 281 Woodcuts. 2 vols. Cloth, gilt top. 20s. *net.*

MANUALS OF CATHOLIC PHILOSOPHY.

(Stonyhurst Series.)

EDITED BY RICHARD F. CLARKE, S.J.

Logic. By RICHARD F. CLARKE, S.J. Crown 8vo. 5s.

First Principles of Knowledge. By JOHN RICKABY, S.J. Crown 8vo. 5s.

Moral Philosophy (Ethics and Natural Law). By JOSEPH RICKABY, S.J. Crown 8vo. 5s.

General Metaphysics. By JOHN RICKABY, S.J. Crown 8vo. 5s.

Psychology. By MICHAEL MAHER, S.J. Crown 8vo. 6s. 6d.

Natural Theology. By BERNARD BOEDDER, S.J. Crown 8vo. 6s. 6d.

Political Economy. By CHARLES S. DEVAS. Crown 8vo. 6s. 6d.

LONDON AND NEW YORK : LONGMANS, GREEN, & CO.
5000/2/93